PRAISE FOR *A PASSION FOR THE POSSIBLE*

"Jean Houston in her brilliant, poignant style has written a masterpiece of a spiritual guide book that helps to remove our ego resistance to the power of love and the passion for life that is in each of us."

—Gerald G. Jampolsky, M.D., author of *Love Is Letting Go of Fear*

"Jean Houston, with passion and innocence, helps one see life in wondrous new ways."

—Mario Puzo, author of *The Godfather* and *The Last Don*

"Jean Houston is a national treasure. She writes from her heart directly to mine—very simply. I love this book."

—Dr. Wayne W. Dyer, author of *Manifest Your Destiny*

"Jean Houston eloquently reveals the Essential Self—the guide within us all, which can lead us to our higher destiny, expose our purpose for being, and manifest all that we can be . . . if we have the courage to listen."

—James Redfield, author of *The Celestine Prophecy*

"With elegant simplicity, Jean Houston shows you how to unleash the genius that lies in the depths of your being."

—Deepak Chopra, author of *The Seven Spiritual Laws of Success*

"Jean Houston, like an archaeologist of the human spirit probing the great myths and mysteries, continues to remind us why we are here on this earth now and why we must not take one moment of our lives for granted."

—Armand Assante, actor, star of *The Odyssey*

"*A Passion for the Possible* is a guide to expressing our fullest potential as human beings by one of the greatest teachers of this time, or indeed, of any time. Jean Houston's work is a blessing in the true sense of the word; it encourages hidden potential to germinate and come to fullest flower."

—Joan Borysenko, author of *Minding the Body, Mending the Mind*

"Jean Houston brings down fire from heaven to empower and inspire individual lives."

—Larry Dossey, M.D. author of *Healing Words* and *Be Careful What You Pray For . . . You Just Might Get It*

A Passion
for the
Possible

*A Guide to Realizing
Your True Potential*

Jean Houston

HarperOne
An Imprint of HarperCollinsPublishers

Grateful acknowledgment is made to the following for permission to reprint previously published material: Bear & Co. for lines from *Meditations with Hildegard of Bingen*, by Gabrielle Uhlein. Copyright © 1983, Bear & Co., Santa Fe, NM. Excerpt from "The Dry Salvages" in *Four Quartets*, copyright © 1941 by T. S. Eliot and renewed 1969 by Esme Valerie Eliot. Reprinted by permission of Harcourt Brace & Company and Faber & Faber Ltd. Jean Houston and Howard Jerome for lyrics to "You Are More!" Copyright © 1979 by Jean Houston. Oriah Mountain Dreamer for permission to reprint "The Invitation" from *Dreams of Desire*. Oriah Mountain Dreamer is a writer, teacher, and workshop facilitatior. She can be reached at 300 Coswell Avenue, Box 22546, Toronto, Ontario, M4L 2A0, Canada. Rumi quotations are from Annemarie Schimmel, *The Triumphal Sun: A Study of the Works of Jalaloddin Rumi* (London and the Hague: East-West Publications, 1980).

HarperCollins books may be purchased for educational, business, or sales promotional use. For information please write: Special Markets Department, HarperCollins Publishers, 10 East 53rd Street, New York, NY 10022.

HarperCollins Web site: http://www.harpercollins.com

HarperCollins®, 📖®, and HarperOne™ are trademarks of HarperCollins Publishers.

FIRST HARPERCOLLINS PAPERBACK EDITION PUBLISHED IN 1998

Library of Congress Cataloging-in-Publication Data
Houston, Jean.

    A passion for the possible : a guide to realizing your true potential /
Jean Houston. — 1st ed.
      p. cm.
    ISBN: 978-0-06-251532-2
    1. Self-actualization (Psychology). I. Title.
BF637.S4H677   1997
158.1—dc21   97–20406

12 13 14 15 16 RRD(H) 20 19 18

For Catherine Tatge,
Dominique Lasseur, and
Kenneth Cavander,
Partners in the Possible

and for Paula Perlis
who understands food
on all four levels

CONTENTS

AN INVITATION TO DISCOVER MORE OF WHAT YOU ARE

You! I know you.

You may not think I know you, but I do.

You are a seeker. You are a fledgling ready to take flight. You sense intuitively that you have potential that you've barely begun to tap. You are a bud ready to blossom. A chrysalis waiting to become a butterfly.

I've met you in the supermarket when you were corralling two energetic kids and pushing a cart full of groceries. I saw you glance longingly at the book rack. Your face had the determined look of someone who knows there's more to life than frozen food and runny noses.

Thirty-five thousand feet up in the air, I've been your seatmate. You told me that your twelve-year-old son pitched a two-hitter last night while you were in a hotel room a thousand miles away. You said that your dream was to quit your sales job and open a woodworking shop in the town where you live.

I've listened as you've told me about discovering that you're a writer. Though all you've got to show for your efforts is a notebook full of unpublished stories and a shoe box full of rejection letters, you're hard at work on the outline of a novel.

I've encountered you as a young college graduate with the world open before you. You are filled with ideals, skills, and dreams but have not yet figured out how to harness that energy—not to mention pay for that student loan.

You came to tell me how it is to be a cancer survivor. You are alive and glad to be so. Your longtime partner couldn't stand hospitals and left you in the middle of chemotherapy, but you have joined a survivors' group and are in training to counsel other cancer patients.

You were the fifty-something woman at my seminar whose youngest daughter had just gone off to college. Though your husband says that "personal fulfillment" is a bunch of baloney, you've signed up for an evening course in world religions and several seminars in addition to mine. "It's my turn now," you told me. "I've come here to find out what's next."

Whoever you are, whatever your life may be, I know you as I know myself. We both face the same challenges. We are living in a time of the most far-reaching and rapid change in human history.

Most of us will log five to fifty times the experience of our ancestors of two hundred years ago. Many of them received at birth the pattern for their lives, growing up to be farmer, weaver, soldier, priest, or mother bearing and burying one baby after another. Rich or poor, peasant or aristocrat, their lives followed the same formulas as had their parents' for ages past. There were advantages, of course. They knew who they were, what to tell their children, the comfort of sameness, and a lack of options.

And then it all changed. It has been said that as many events have happened from 1945 to today as have happened in the two thousand years before 1945. The ancient curse "may you live in interesting times" has come true for us. This is it—the most interesting time in human history. Nothing comparable has happened to humankind since the industrial revolution or, further back, since we gave up the wanderings of the hunt and settled down to agriculture and civilization.

Our everyday lives reflect this quantum leap in the complexity and pace of contemporary experience. We are caught uncertain, unprepared, and unprotected in the face of too much happening too often. We are the people of the parenthesis, at the end of one era and not quite at the beginning of the new one. Some of us withdraw from the onslaught. We become workaholics. Or we find numbing solace in addictions or in hours spent staring at the television. Too many of us agree to lives of serial monotony and the progressive dimming of our passion for life.

But many, a significant number, are trying to understand the momentous opportunity that is ours. The future

3

is seeded in the time of parenthesis. We are among the most important people who have ever lived. We will determine whether humankind will grow or die, evolve or perish.

How do we prepare ourselves for such times? How do we prepare ourselves to take responsibility for the personal as well as the planetary process? We have not been trained for this task, and the usual formulas and stopgap solutions will not help us. The density and intimacy of the global village, the staggering consequences of our new knowledge and technologies make us directors of a world that, up to now, has mostly directed us.

Today our extremely limited human consciousness has powers over life and death that once mythically were accorded to the "gods." Extremely limited consciousness with the press of a button can launch a nuclear holocaust. Extremely limited consciousness intervenes in the genetic code, interferes with the complex patterns in the sea and on the land, and pours wastes into the Earth's protective ozone layers, wiping out countless plant and animal species. Extremely limited consciousness has killed 100 million humans in the last sixty years.

Extremely limited consciousness gives us governments that are too large for the small problems of life and too small in spirit for the large problems. Extremely limited consciousness cannot deal with ethnic and tribal violence and the rage of the dispossessed, the addiction to consumption and soul-killing substances, the very survival of life on this planet. Instead, extremely limited consciousness offers

4

us a patchwork quilt of solutions that create ten new problems for each quick fix.

What qualities of mind, body, and spirit can overcome
these limitations? How do we go about preparing ourselves
to become stewards of the planet, filled with enough passion for the possible to partner one another through the
greatest social transformation ever known?

This book is about discovering and developing these
qualities. It is about our natural ability to gain a passion for
the possible through the greater use of our innate potentials.
Only in this way can we can rise to the challenge of our
times and ferry ourselves across the dangerous waters sepa-
rating a dying era from one being born. Regardless of how
unfulfilled our lives may seem, regardless of how meager
our self-esteem, we are called into greatness by the necessity
of our age, and we have little choice but to say yes.

You may be thinking that this is an impossible task. We all
feel inadequate when it comes to stopping the flood of world-
destroying problems or to growing beyond our personal limitations. I know the despair I feel when watching the evening
news or reading the morning paper. And from firsthand
experience I know how the media distorts the truth of things
in order to get a selling story, torching lives and careers in the
process. I often feel my own inadequacy to serve my world
and time as I wish to do before I die. And I can relate to those
of you who also feel that time is running out if we are going
to make a difference and make a better world.

But then I vividly remember, as I am sure you do, seeing
the picture of the Earth from outer space for the first time.

To many of the Earth's peoples, seeing our planet floating in space activated something very deep in the human spirit. Suddenly we realized that we belong to a much larger unity of life and of peoples. After seeing that picture of Home, we began to cherish the whole planet, not just our particular part or nation. We began to understand that one part of the world can no longer dominate the others through economic or military strength.

In the midst of the turmoil of too-rapid change, an extraordinary light has arisen. Factors unique in human history are poised to help us become more than we thought we ever could be. We glimpse in the next century the coming of a planetary society, which heralds the end of ancient enmities and the birth of new ways of using our common humanity and its various cultures. In fact, we will need a gathering of the potentials of the whole human race and the particular genius of every culture if we are going to survive our time.

Part of my work has been studying cultural potentials and harvesting them for use in education, health care, social welfare, personal growth, work, art, and creativity. I have found that challenges that arise in one culture can often be met by applying strategies developed in another.

In a tribe in West Africa, for example, community issues are looked at in ways that we would find astonishing. The question—say, improving waste disposal in the village—is presented in a village meeting. Then people dance the problem, sing about it, draw it in the sand, close their eyes and imagine solutions, sleep and dream about it, dance some more, and then suddenly—a solution! And a very good one, too, for people have run the problem through many different modes of knowing and have looked at it from many different points of view.

How paltry our endless committee meetings and position papers seem compared to this! In fact, why don't you try it some time? When you seek a solution to something that concerns you—say, the garbage that pours into your children's minds as they watch television—don't just sit there and frown. Dance, drum, imagine, invoke, invite, draw, sing the issue. And see what happens.

The world's peoples have many other good and useful ideas. In Bali people learn artistic crafts very quickly by first entering into the interior sense of "being" a complex dance, a mask, a statue, a painting and only then expressing what they "are" in physical form.

Among the Inuit peoples of northern Canada and Alaska, the way to fix a mechanical problem is intuited by the mechanic, who closes his eyes and walks through the faulty engine in his mind. He developed this expertise in visualizing because his people have learned to hold in their minds an inner map of the subtle details of a landscape that can disappear in snow from one moment to the next.

In Turkey, dervishes whose whirling dance is a form of prayer have found the sounds and movements that take them to a state of union with the One.

We, too, in the West are contributing an essential element to the coming world culture. Western women are leading the way toward the rise of women around the

7

world to full partnership with men in virtually the entire domain of human affairs. And as women are being equally empowered, men are being freed to discover that activities often seen as "feminine"—feeling, nurturing, collaboration, celebration, relationships—are in fact the domain of all. Personally, I believe this to be the most important change in human history.

The rich mind style of women, which has been gestating in the womb of preparatory time, lo, these many millennia is catching on, and with it comes a tremendous change in the way we do things.

Women emphasize process more than product; their special gift is making things cohere, relate, grow. Through women's eyes, relationships are more important than final outcomes. The world within is as important as the world without. Governance, games, education, work, health, society itself are held to new standards that honor the fullness of who and what we can be.

This is a tremendous change, and once it is in full flower, the world will have turned a corner.

In the new world that lies just ahead, all of these individual skills and fresh solutions will be needed to face the perils and harvest the promise of a technology and media-driven world. People and ideas are fast becoming interconnected in ways that create a new environment—virtually a new world mind.

The challenge is in figuring out how our local minds can hope to cope with the resulting overload of information. Too many people are already drowning in the glut. Some waste hours on the internet, withdrawn from friends and family, cluttering up their heads with life-leeching trivia.

But others have found ideas and communities on-line that feed their minds, giving them courage to take on projects they never would have dreamed possible. A fourteen-year-old girl I know of used the internet from her home in New England to help organize a movement to clean up the oceans!

It is as if a worldwide nervous system is in the works. Each of us is a brain cell in that system, with powers that once belonged to kings.

How do we train ourselves to live in an interconnected world, an ever-changing world, a world in which the unexpected is the expected and the breakdown and reconstruction of everything we ever knew is daily fare? We are attending a vast wake for a way of being that has been ours for hundreds, even thousands, of years.

But we are also the ones who will carry on. We have an unparalleled opportunity to cultivate the human capacities that we need to deal with the opening times that follow upon closing times. The good news is that our bodies and minds are coded with an extraordinary array of possibilities and potentials. The bad news is that we learn to use very few of them.

It is as if we were a musical instrument with a million keys, but we tootle and hoot on only some twenty of them. The stupendous music of our minds goes largely unplayed and unknown.

It is as if we are living in the middle of a vast garden

filled with wonderful fruits and vegetables, starving because we eat only the bugs we find on the ground.

Existing on so narrow a band has brought frustration and misery, the shadow of hate and the threat of apocalypse. Our current ecological catastrophe has been engendered by the gross overuse of the outward world and the terrible underuse of the inner world.

As Jesus says in the gnostic Gospel of Thomas, "If you bring forth what is within you, what you bring forth will save you. If you do not bring forth what is within you, what you do not bring forth will destroy you."

In this time of whole-system transition we can no longer afford to live as half-light versions of ourselves. The complexity of our time requires a greater and wiser use of our capacities, a rich playing of the instrument we have been given. The world can thrive only if we can grow. The possible society can become a reality only if we learn to be the possible humans we are meant to be.

I recently asked an audience what capacities they felt they needed to deal with this challenge. One woman said that what she needed most was courage—courage to reorder her priorities and make time for personal exploration instead of dedicating her best hours to work and the promise of outward success.

Another talked of learning new strategies for accomplishing the multiple tasks that were her lot. She held a full-time job while taking care of her home and family while going to school to complete a graduate degree in social work while being responsible for her aged parents.

Yet another spoke of finding ways to maintain the best possible health in the face of her complex and busy life.

During the break, a number of people came up to me with ideas. One woman spoke of feeling a push from the past and a pull from the future to be all that she could be. "It's as if my ancestors demand it, and my descendants require it."

A man reported that the capacity he most desired was to reactivate the parts of himself he had let lapse.

"Like what?" I asked.

"Like memory, imagination, creativity," he replied. "I've been running so hard, I've forgotten who I am. As a young man I was filled with dreams and ideas—so many ideas. I want to get some of them back."

Human beings are not constituted to be content with living as thwarted, inhibited versions of themselves. Throughout history and all over the world, people have felt a yearning to be more, a longing to push the membrane of the possible. They have entered monasteries and mystery schools, pursuing secular as well as esoteric studies. They have practiced yoga, martial arts, sports, dance, art. They have left home and family to adventure beyond the ordinary, embarking on visionary and spiritual quests.

These pursuits come with the territory of being human. It is as if there are catalytic agents cooking in our genes that regularly sputter and pop with evolutionary juices. "It is time to wake up now," they seem to say.

And so I ask you to reflect on this: What would you be like if you started today to make the most of the rest of your life? If you turned a corner and awoke?

Suddenly, you are intensely connected with all the inner wisdom you contain, more present and alive in this moment than you have been in the previous drowse of many years. Each day brings new thoughts and feelings or interesting variations on old ones. No longer is 90 percent of what you think and feel the same as what you thought and felt yesterday or will think and feel tomorrow.

Many of the so-called larger-than-life people differ from the rest of us chiefly in this respect: It is not that they are actually larger in mind and soul or more brilliant. Rather, they are profoundly present to the stuff of their lives, to what is happening within themselves as well as around them.

They use and enjoy their senses more, they inhabit with keen awareness their bodies as well as their minds, they explore the world of imagery and imagination, they rehearse memories, engage in projects that reinvent the world, are serious about life but laugh at themselves, and seek to empower others as they would be empowered. Quite simply, they are cooking on more burners. And when at last they lie dying, they can say, "Life has been an eminently satisfactory experience."

My work is to show people how to wake up, how to inhabit parts of themselves that have been left vacant and unexplored. We are told in Christian scripture that "In my Father's house there are many mansions." As above, so below. In the province of the human condition, there are countless houses, apartments, condominiums, tents, and even a few mansions, many of which have been uninhabited for years.

When we move out of the cardboard box we have called home and take up residence in some of these glorious places, our reality heightens dramatically. We begin to live with everyday passion. Things become more real. Colors and shapes and ideas and relationships have more intensity, energy, and pattern.

This acuity brings with it a motivation to "get on with it." Old obstructions dissolve as we discover new ways of being, new forms of enterprise—a new body and a new mind.

IT'S TIME TO WAKE UP!

A friend, Howard Jerome, and I once wrote a rousing song complete with drums and trumpets and an ascending melody that tried to convey the untapped potential we each contain. It is called "You Are More!" Here are the words:

You are more than you pretend to be
You are more than what most eyes can see
You are more than all your history
Look inside and you will find
There's glory in your mind
Come be the kind of person you would be. . . .

You are more than what your leaders say
You are more than how you earn your pay
You are more than what you seem today
So drop that loser's mask

You're equal to the task
The question you should ask is who you are. . . .

You are more than what the preachers shout
You are more, come let your spirit out
You are more, your soul shall have no doubt
Arise, become awake
With every breath you take
The god within will ache to be. . . .

You are more than cell and blood and bone
You are more than just your name alone
You are more than all that you may own
Look around you everywhere
There's something that we share
The magic in the air is you!

You are more than some statistic chart
You are more than the sum of all your parts
You are more inside your heart of hearts
You know that it is true
This being that is you
Has miracles to do
Believe. . . .

Believe that you are more, that you contain an inner self, a true self, that can emerge only if you give it attention. You might consider it the fetus of your Higher Self, an evolutionary being ready to be born.

Much of the urgency that you have felt these last years—moving between stress and distress, the sense of living in an outmoded condition, the exhilaration before what is not yet, the dread of leaving the womb of the old era—comes from the birth pangs of a social evolution that is upon us.

Birth is a journey. Second birth is as great a journey. Thus the recurring theme in many of the world's scriptures, "Unless you be born again you cannot enter the Kingdom. . . ."

New birth requires new being. It means laying down new pathways in the senses to take in the news of this remarkable world. It means extending the field of your psychology so that there is more of you to do so much of this. New birth demands that you choose a richer, juicier story, even a new myth, by which to comprehend your life and that you begin to live out of it. And most important of all, it asks that you be sourced and re-sourced in God, Spirit—the Love that moves the sun and all the stars.

In what follows, we will begin to seek these pathways, fields, stories, sources. I will be your guide, your friend of the road. Together we will journey into four levels of self, four extraordinary worlds, each with its own treasures and powers.

Through decades of research and teaching, I have found that all human beings contain these inner realms, but few have more than a passing acquaintance with what they hold. Most are familiar with only the surface dimensions, leaving their inward reaches unexplored.

Yet it is in the world within that these realms of being have their greatest range, variety, and depth. In them lie

15

dormant potentials. In them are the materials for reweaving mind and body. From them you get marching orders for your soul's deepest purpose. From them you begin again!

What are these familiar yet alien realms?

The most accessible is the sensory, physical realm, the level of the body and the senses. Next is the psychological realm, the level of personal history and emotions. The third I call the mythic and symbolic realm, the level of story and of universal patterns. The deepest, the spiritual realm, is the Great Mystery out of which we all emerge.

Before we begin our exploration, let me advise you that the power of this book resides in reimagining your practice of reading. The technique I have in mind is not unfamiliar. When we read novels and stories, we often find ourselves seeing with an inner eye and hearing with an inner ear the characters and events described. If the book is especially engaging, the storied world may for a time seem even more real to us than our "real life" surroundings.

Although this is not a novel, it is an adventure that asks that you be a conscious participant in an unfolding drama. As we travel through these pages together, I will often suggest things for you to think about and do that can help you experience potentials in each of the four realms. I invite you to imagine them as vividly as you can, for in imagination lies the key to discovery.

You will be eating ripe peaches and walking on warm beaches in the sensory realm. In the psychological realm you will meet members of your inner crew—elder, child, mechanic, poet. In the realm of myth, you will travel to a

16

time long, long ago in a galaxy far away with a number of familiar characters. Finally, in the spiritual realm you will come Home to who and what you really are.

We will use words as wands to evoke the inner self of your potential being. By the end of the book you will discover that you have grown new sides to yourself, a stronger sense of your own essence, and a passion to live out your possibilities.

You may even have to look in the mirror and reintroduce yourself!

Let us begin our journey by making a quick trip to the four realms, just to get a sense of the lay of the land. After that, we will take a more extensive voyage of discovery into the hidden reaches and secret byways of each dimension of our being. Ready? Let's go on a scouting mission to the four levels of inner space.

17

A Journey to the Four Levels of Your Being

What is it that allows some people to tap into their creative power and do wonders in music, art, literature, and science, while others flounder in despair and confusion, cut off from the creator within?

What is it that allows some people to see each problem as "an opportunity in work clothes," while others hide from the challenges that confront them or numb themselves to their impact?

I once made a study of fifty-five of the most creative people in America, innovators like Margaret Mead, Joseph Campbell, Linus Pauling, Jonas Salk, and Buckminster Fuller. Each had sustained a high level of inquiry and discovery in her or his field over many years.

Though very different in personality and interests, these creative geniuses, I found, had one important thing in common. They were each familiar with their interior world and believed that its ideas and images could spark their projects. Each had become an archaeologist of the mind, a spelunker in the cave of inner inspiration.

Some felt that delving into the depths of their own being was like getting in touch with the forms and patterns of Creation itself.

A scientist at the Rockefeller Institute who was part of the study said to me, "I feel sometimes as if I am tapping into the warehouse of God. I know my science, of course, and when I go inside, I find many of my own ideas and concepts all got up in symbols and fancy dress, and that's tremendous fun. But when I go deeper, it seems as if the ideas are coming from some other place. It's not just that they are richer and more elegant, but occasionally quite beyond anything I had ever thought of. Then I wonder, 'Who is the who that thought of that?'"

Who indeed? I have long pondered that scientist's question. In that regard, I am in fine company. Francis of Assisi once said, "What we are looking for is Who is looking."

The great German mystic Meister Eckhart put it even more plainly, "The eye by which I see God is the same eye by which God sees me."

We are not "encapsulated bags of skin dragging around a dreary little ego," as my late friend Alan Watts so whimsically put it. Instead, each of us is a little world, complete with organisms and environments. That little world—each human being—is nested within the greater Environment of Being, which it both contains and mimics.

Our bodies are of the stuff of stars and the minerals of Earth. Our blood runs briny with the seas, and we ourselves are living planets for billions of little beings, microorganisms and who knows what else. Our genes are universes in themselves, coded with enough information to recreate the world.

Our cells contain the memories of all things past—the birth of stars, the coming of life, the experience of being fish and amphibian, reptile and early mammal, monkey and human, and the lure now calling us from beyond the horizon to enter the next stage of our becoming.

Perhaps, then, it is the "nature that lies within"—the inner mirror of the Great Nature pushing the universe along on its evolutionary journey—that is the "who" calling us to be more than we ever thought we could be. Physicists know this force as the "strange attractor," the universal principle by which increasing complexity produces beauty. In human terms, it is our lure toward a destiny beyond our present knowings.

That which we call God may have much greater plans for us than we could ever imagine. Of course, we have the freedom to accept or reject these plans. We can choose to cocreate with the Creator, or we can deny our inheritance and let our lives bumble along until they are finished.

We all know lives that seem unplugged, disconnected from all that gives existence vitality and meaning. Maybe we have even lived such lives ourselves. It is not that we are actually cut off from the Source. It's just that we have lived as if that were the case, until a fortress of forgetfulness grows up around our consciousness.

Our responsibility—our capacity to respond to the challenges that face us, our *response ability*—is to reconnect with the larger Source that we sometimes call divine. When we do so, we reconnect with the energy and the plan for our larger life and all that it entails.

Reconnection means laying down pathways to the Source in whatever way is right for us—meditation, prayer, dancing exuberantly, walking in the woods. We are as different as snowflakes, and our ways to the Source reflect this. We live in what is perhaps the first time in history when people are free to explore their own pathways. But like a new trail blazed through the forest, the path we choose must be traveled often before it becomes useful and familiar.

Going to church every Sunday is a time-honored way of reconnecting with the Source on a regular basis so that a Sunday spirit infuses our weekdays. Buddhism teaches people to apply the insights gained on the meditation cushion to each ordinary event and encounter. Sufis learn to inhabit the realms within—the *Alam al Mithal*—so that they can bring what they find there to the world without. Eventually the worlds within and without are recognized as inseparable parts of the One Reality in which we live and move and have our being.

These and many other pathways to traditional wisdom are readily available today through books, seminars, and retreats. With such an embarrassment of riches, some of us are easily seduced into become spiritual dilettantes—enjoying the appetizers but never making a full meal of sacred food.

We all know "spiritual shoppers" who work their way through a supermarket full of traditional and nontraditional choices—a Catholic mass here, a Native American sweat lodge there, Sufi dancing, Kabbalah study with a rabbi, darshan from a visiting Hindu guru, a few sessions with a Jungian analyst, and a meditation retreat with a Tibetan lama. And still they're anxious!

It is important to investigate the forms and practices of the inner life, but once you discover what truly draws you to the Source, you would do best to explore it for some time. Real growth comes with going deeply into an authentic spiritual path and sticking with it through its rewards and difficulties, not from gathering spiritual pollen like some fickle honeybee.

Whatever your predilection or disposition, whether you hail from Southeast Asia or southwest Texas, whatever your culture or profession, you will find means and methods that lead you to the Source in the explorations that follow. Though not a spiritual path in themselves, these excursions into the interior of your being can help you to discover the path that is authentically yours or to connect more deeply with the path you have already inherited or chosen.

Reconnecting to the Source does not need to be a mysterious process. Let me give you an everyday example. Recently I had to renew and update the access codes on the receiver of my home satellite dish. If I had not installed new codes, the hundreds of television stations moving through the airwaves would be blocked, and I would see only seven channels.

Each of us has access codes to the many stations of our being. Our tendency is to forget to update them and to tune ourselves day after day to the same old programs. And yet the reality waves that move through us are filled with extraordinary stories and ideas, even connection to the ultimate Program, the greatest show in the universe. When we renew our access codes, the static clears, we get messages from the Source, and we are retuned and coded for the life we were meant to live.

The world within, which contains these codes, has been called many things. Saint Teresa of Avila termed it the Interior Castle. Trappist monk and mystic Thomas Merton spoke of the Seven-Storied Mountain. Psychologists talk about the personal and collective unconscious. If you're a computer type, you might think of it as the great meta-computer within. In *The Wizard of Oz,* Dorothy calls it "our own backyard."

Meditators and mystics, healers and helpers, visionaries and creators from every walk of life have always visited the wonders of inner space. Our enduring fascination with dreams testifies to the power of inner imagery to entertain and to inform. Imagine, then, how much more useful it will be to learn ways to explore our interior geography while awake and conscious.

In my Mother/Father's house are many mansions. Growth requires that we set up housekeeping in rooms that have largely been uninhabited by our conscious minds.

So many realities lie within that it would be impossible to explore them all in this book. To whet your appetite for inner adventuring, we will concentrate on the four major levels I have found to be present whenever I have taken depth soundings of the human psyche—the sensory, psychological, mythic, and spiritual levels.

Though the details of the inner world vary in content and emphasis from one culture to the next, their main features and basic themes are similar. In workshops I have led the world over, people have used these simple techniques to gain a passion for the possible and to commit more of themselves to making a better world.

A Brahmin woman in India used these methods to set up a center in which Shudra women (the caste known as the Untouchables) learn skills and find self-esteem and gainful employment. A Texas woman inspired by this work created what she calls a "Listening Tree," where people are heard deeply and then guided to become much more than they thought they were. In Burma, a Catholic priest and a Buddhist monk I have worked with have joined forces to try to create a freer society.

You can vary the techniques I offer according to your own beliefs and preferences. The law in all of my work is "be creative." Find new and better ways of doing the processes I suggest. Your inner wisdom knows how to do this. Make my methods your own.

Some of the methods I suggest will seem very familiar. Others may seem strange. All that is required is that you imagine as vividly as you can the experiences and sensations

I suggest. Also, I ask that as you read you make a special effort to focus your attention and concentration.

As words on the page guide you on this inner journey, you may find it useful at times to close your eyes after you have read a suggestion so that you can explore more fully the realm you are investigating. Soon you will learn how to stay as mindful in the inner world as you often are in the outer one.

Of course you can also keep your eyes open throughout. Try it both ways and see what best suits you. Even if you do not immediately experience the world I am describing, act as if you do. That will often serve to prime the pump of the imagination.

Ready? Let's begin.

I ask you to imagine that you are climbing a spiral path up a small mountain. You smell the pine trees, feel the crunch of leaves and pine needles under your feet. You hear birdsong all around and the soughing of the wind in the trees. Glimpses of blue sky and dappling sunlight break through openings in the treetops. A cold clear stream courses down the hill, and you cup some water in your hand to quench your thirst.

Paying full attention to these surroundings, continue to walk up and around the path that leads you up the mountain.

Now you hear a mighty shriek, look up, and see an eagle flying overhead, riding the air currents. You take this for good sign, and although you may be tiring, you keep on walking up and around, around and up, keeping on going up and up and around, following the spiraling path up the mountain.

You reach the top, where the mountain narrows almost to a point. Here you discover lying flat on the ground a stone tablet inscribed with symbols. They may not be readable now, but perhaps later they will convey some message to you. It seems to you that the tablet is covering something. With effort, you lift the tablet and move it off to the side.

You see now an entrance into the interior of the mountain, just wide enough to squeeze through. You climb inside and almost immediately find yourself on another path, this one taking you down and around the inside of the mountain. Although this place is strange, it soon begins to feel very familiar to you. This is as it should be, for this is the home for all that you are or could be.

Although it is dark here, a subtle light emanates from the walls, allowing you to see. As you continue down the path, you notice a door in the wall, the first you have seen. A shiny brass plaque identifies it as the door to the Realm of the Senses.

You move closer, drawn by the interesting smells that seem to emanate from the door—cinnamon and lavender and hot buttered popcorn. You notice that the panels of the door are made of different sensory delights. One is chocolate mousse. Scoop some out with your fingers if you like. Another is a patchwork of interesting textures—velvets and silks and the bark of a tree. From another a rock band seems to be playing.

Of course, these sensations are just suggestions. Your sensory doorway may be made up of different tastes, sounds, sights, and smells. Let's open the door now and find out what lies within.

A stun of color! Cascades of sound! Every sensation is so fresh and vibrant it seems as if you are walking in the world on the first day of Creation. The music smells of flowers. Aromas embrace you. There are smells that would be gardens, symphonies of perfume and spice.

You know things in ways you haven't known them before. Looking at the whorl of a flower, you are carried down into the spiral of its growth, all the way down to its original seed. Touch a tree, and sense through your fingertips its living presence, the photosynthesis in its leaves, the slow burrowing of its roots.

A tray appears with exquisite crystal goblets. Each is filled with a liquid radiant with a particular color. Each color is the very essence of itself. As you drink the elixir from the blue goblet, the yellow goblet, the green goblet, the purple, orange, and violet goblets, you experience what it is to be these colors, to be blue and yellow and green and purple and orange and violet.

As you walk along you discover that you have become more supple. You move with fluidity and grace, each muscle and joint and cell having remembered its optimal form. You are delighted to be in your body.

You are drawn to all that lies before you—flocks of

27

gorgeous orange and black monarch butterflies and age-less, elegantly draped willow trees, an ancient boulder, a babbling brook, an arbor of lush purple grapes. All around you is a light that feels loving, and that sensation of love is reflected in everything you experience—a misty dawn, the blackness of seeds in the flesh of a watermelon, the salt smell of a sea breeze.

Close your eyes and get in touch with the world of sensory memory and imagination that lies within you. Take other paths, try out new and old scenes, discover the delicious wonders that are waiting for you there. A special quality of happiness comes with discovering the vast sensory world that you can visit without having to go anywhere at all.

28 | It is time to move on to another level of the world within. Know, however, that you can return to the sensory realm and explore it further whenever you wish. But let us leave now, going back through the sensory door and closing it behind us.

Back on the spiral path once again, you brush the walls with your outstretched hands as you find your way down and around, deeper and deeper into the interior of the mountain.

Suddenly you see a glint of light. Another doorway is before you. Its shiny surface is a mirror. It is the entrance to the Realm of the Psyche, the psychological level—the world of individual and collective memory and feeling.

You move closer. At first the mirror seems ordinary enough, but then the reflection dissolves, and you see images of yourself at different ages—as a baby, a child, a teenager, your present age, and even much older than you are now.

The mirror clouds and becomes clear again.

Now you see yourself in other times in history, perhaps even in other body forms: An Inuit next to an igloo. A tall African woman carrying a large jug of water on her head. A Renaissance prince in the court of the Medici. A Japanese Samurai warrior. An Egyptian priestess in a linen shift and black wig. A Bedouin in hooded cloak, face muffled against the desert sand. A pioneer woman in a covered wagon.

Keep looking in the mirror to see what figures emerge for you. . . .

Now you open the mirrored door and enter. A little ways down the path, you come upon a still pond fringed with foliage. It is the pool of memory. Memories of childhood emerge from the waters—favorite foods, friends, games, trips, treats, parents, teachers, pets. Memories of later times in your life—the first time you fell in love. A recent birthday party. A new job or enterprise. A time when you exceeded what you thought you could do.

You pick up a pebble that is close at hand and throw it into the pond. A circle appears, which shows a scene from your childhood—perhaps the moment when you read your first word. The expanding rings reveal the impact that moment had on the rest of your life.

Throw another pebble and watch the rippling effect of an incident from another time in your life. Another pebble, another incident.

The rings now cross each other, and you begin to sense the interconnections between the events of your life. You might start to see your personal history as a series of linking patterns or rhythms. Discovering the patterns that are uniquely yours is a key that opens up many possibilities. With this perspective, you can more easily take the helm and direct your life toward patterns more likely to bring you joy than sorrow.

In the psychological realm, the past is never finished and the present is never fixed. You can even embark upon a kind of time travel here, journeying backward and forward in time to heal old wounds and transform obstacles into opportunities.

Like the flashing of a goldfish beneath the water, a memory slips into awareness—a time when you really needed a good friend or adviser. You see yourself, younger than you are now, a child, perhaps, who needs comfort or empowerment. You can reach out to that child now and offer the friendship and recognition that would have meant so much.

Knowing that you can return to the pool of memory at any time, leave it now and begin to walk through the dark of the forest.

You come to a large clearing, where it is light again. You enter the center of a circle of friendly people. Although you may have never have seen them before, they seem curiously familiar. That is because they are aspects of yourself. You might call them your inner crew. They have gathered here to offer you the opportunity to take better advantage of their talents and gifts.

Look around the circle and see who is there. One might be a healer, a person who knows a great deal about getting and keeping you healthy. Perhaps a cook is there, too, and an accountant, an athlete, and a mechanic.

You have a vast crew within you, and among them is the one who pays bills, the hard worker, the one who knows how to relax, the loving one, the one who can rise to righteous anger, the masculine aspect of yourself, the feminine aspect of yourself, the clown, the child, the wise old one, the hero or heroine, the social activist, the meditator, the writer, the inventor.

You even have a priest or priestess inside and also one with the gift for friendship and relationship, one who knows how to use time, one who has the gift of spiritual awakening. Each of these inner selves comes forward now and shakes your hand or embraces you and tells you the gift she or he brings you.

31

As each one touches you, you feel the charge of that self's unique gift—a kaleidoscope of genius, sequences of mastery.

"All these capacities are yours," they say.

"But what about things I can't do?" you ask. "Like painting or house building or poetry?"

A reply comes. "If you wish to study these things, call upon the master builder or poet or painter within to help you. Your studies will go further and faster than you might have expected."

Suddenly, you become aware of a presence that all the other selves regard with awe and respect. This being looks like you, but a you who has evolved into all that you could be. This presence is sometimes called the Daimon—the activating intelligence that guides your life. You might think of it as your Essential Self. When you enter consciously into close relationship with this presence, your life takes on purpose and energy. You know what you have to do in this world.

With a long look of deep appreciation at this wonderful being and a whispered vow to meet again soon, you turn and walk out of the clearing, following the path back through the forest.

Knowing that there are many more wonders to explore in the Realm of the Psyche, you leave it now, closing the mirrored door behind you.

Once again you are on the spiral path that leads you down and around. You descend, more confident now, until you come to a heavy wooden door ingeniously carved with symbols: a Cross and the Star of David. The half-black, half-white circle of Yin and Yang. The painted shields of Native American peoples.

It is the door to the Realm of Myth and Symbol, and these symbols represent the myths and stories of many cultures and many times. You notice the curious looped cross called the Ankh, the symbol of life for ancient Egyptians, and the Crescent Moon and Star of Islam.

Pulling open the heavy door, you enter a fantasyland of the mind. All around you, characters from fairy tales are enacting their stories. Here are Snow White and the Seven Dwarfs. Hansel and Gretel are entering a candy and gingerbread house. Aladdin is pursuing adventures with his lamp. Jack is halfway up the beanstalk. Was that Dorothy and her friends, the Scarecrow, the Tin Man, and the Lion, going by?

As you move deeper into this realm, you leave the land of fairy tale and move into the land of myth. You see a tableau of Greek gods feasting on Mount Olympus. The Egyptian goddess Isis searching for her lost husband, Osiris. The Buddha sitting in meditation under the bodhi tree. Sir Percival searching for the Holy Grail. Odysseus eluding the one-eyed Cyclops.

Here are the great and wise feminine characters of myth—Aphrodite rising from the sea on her half-shell, bringing love into the world. White Buffalo Woman gifting the Native American peoples with foodstuffs and ceremony. The Chinese goddess Kwan Yin teaching compassion.

Here too are the characters and events from the new emerging myths—Star Wars' Luke Skywalker and Princess Leia battling the dark forces of the empire.

In the distance is a swirling mist teeming with ever-changing forms. There new myths are coming into being. A charged presence lures you toward it. It is the Daimon, your essential self, the directing presence of your life. You enter the mist, and the presence becomes stronger. Although you hear nothing, you understand that new powers will be opened if you learn to see your own story as a myth.

Suddenly you find yourself on a mythic journey. It begins when you feel called by Someone or Something to leave your old life and journey somewhere new. All your usual delaying tactics rise up to avoid this call. "I'm not ready." "Maybe when the kids are grown." "When I have enough money." But somehow you find the resolve and take the first step.

Soon an ally appears—perhaps an animal to accompany and protect you. A bear? A lion? A dog?

Together you come to a bridge that you must cross. It is the threshold of the realm of amplified power, and it is guarded by a monster who will not let you pass. The monster is fierce, and it reminds you of forces in your life that would keep you stuck in old ways of being.

Your animal friend barks or growls encouragement. Instead of retreating, you confront the monster with a song, a question, a joke, a riddle. It looks amazed, then smiles and invites you to cross the bridge and continue your journey.

34

You walk on until you come to a pyramid. You open a door in the base and follow a long upward path into a chamber where there is a empty sarcophagus—the King's coffin. Something beckons you to lie down in it. You are alone, withdrawn from all that has given you joy. Yet you know that this tomb is also a womb from which you will be birthed to a richer, more complex life. Your gestation complete, you rise and continue your journey.

Now a new ally joins you, a special person from myth or legend with miraculous powers, who becomes your friend and guide. Together you face great challenges and dangers. Do you heal a king, slay a dragon, rescue a captive prince or princess, recover a lost treasure, or face adventures of your own devise? Each challenge leaves you with new powers, new strengths.

After many toils and triumphs, you reach the furthest and deepest point of your journey. A majestic figure beckons. It is your higher parent, the wisdom being who knows who you really are and encourages your finer destiny. As you kneel to receive a blessing, you feel yourself reconciled with all authorities in your life.

You turn now to meet at last the Beloved of the Soul—your angel, your divine other half, your life's spiritual partner. In the Beloved's embrace, all yearnings are fulfilled and you know the wonder of unconditional love. The Beloved gives you a gift—a new idea or life-changing quality with miraculous consequences for you and the world you live in.

And so you and your allies return across the threshold of amplified power. Though your allies depart at the entrance to your everyday world, they let you know that from this moment they live forever within you to give you protection and guidance.

You know, too, that your adventures have given new qualities of courage and mastery to your life, new ways of being and doing in the world. You will return to your ordinary life blessed and gifted, ready and able to make a difference.

You are ready to leave the Realm of Myth and its characters and adventures. You close the carved door of symbols and descend once more on the spiral pathway that takes you down and around the interior mountain. This time the journey down takes much longer, and there are many more turnings on the path.

Finally, you come to a door that seems to be a sheet of shimmering water. It is the entrance to the Realm of the Spirit. You pass through and notice at once a profound difference. Your clothes are immaculate and your mind crystal clear. Though you are drenched, you feel as if you have been washed both inside and out.

Purified and refreshed, you look back at the doorway of water and see only light. It dazzles your eyes and illumines your entire being. Now the light wells up from you as well, and you know the light that is love that is light that is love. The old locks on your heart dissolve, and a tenderness spreads out from your center to enfold all you see in loving communion.

And you see everything. You hear everything. It seems that you are becoming everything. It is as if you have been retuned and can receive the wonders of Creation in all its forms.

You feel an expansion, an amplification, and with it a dissolving of the boundaries of your local self. And yet, at the same time, you are more who you truly are than ever you were.

An energy moves through you that is Creation itself. It is as if you have hitched a ride on the Mind of God and traveled to the State of Grace.

It's all there! The things you have known in your life are experienced in the fullness of their perfection. Cheese is perfect cheese. Music is the melody of life. A friend is the soul's companion.

Think beginnings, and you are present at the birth of a child and the birth of our universe. Think middles, and you witness the child's growth to maturity, the movement of atoms and stars and planets, the evolution of life in its myriad forms. Think endings, and you stand witness to death and our transition into another form and to the passing of old stars into new energies.

Think connection, and you know how it is all related—the cheese, the melody, the friend, the star, the starfish on the beach, the woman passing you in the street, the glint of dust floating in the sun's last ray—all part of a symphony of life in which each part is part of another and part of the whole.

Now you understand the mystic's revelation: "Every creature is a word of God and a book about God." And you know yourself to be a word of God and that within yourself is God's book ready to be read.

What rises from your heart is praise. Praise for the stars, praise for the new corn, praise for the child, praise for the body you inhabit, praise for the gifts you have given and the gifts you have received. Praise for the moon at night and the sun by day. Praise for the one who helps you and the one who does not. Praise for the mystery of your life, praise for the eventuality of death. Praise for all that is and was and shall be.

Finally you enter a sanctuary where there is perfect peace and silence—a silence that is so full that you become the silence, the All, and you know that you have returned Home to the One. And there you rest. . . .

When you feel it is time, you rise to depart, secure in the knowledge that you can come back to this realm whenever you wish, for now you know the way.

Moving back through the door of spiritual water, you remount the steep path up and around the interior mountain. You pass the carved door of mythic symbols and the mirrored door of the world of memory. In the half-light you smell the sweetness of chocolate as you pass the door of the senses.

Again you are on top of the mountain. Replacing the stone tablet, you are once again under the open sky. As you walk down the spiral path, the smell of pine tickles your nose with a sharper freshness, and you revel in the play of winds tossing your hair. Your sight is more acute as well and distinguishes new shadings of green and brown and gray in the trees you pass. At the base of the mountain, perched on a treetop and regarding you with a cool benevolence, is the eagle. You salute him and know yourself to have returned from an extraordinary adventure.

❦ SAVORING THE SENSORY WORLD

Once there was a woman who was without sight or sound. In spite of this, she became a sensory genius. She explained pink as being "like a baby's cheek or a soft southern breeze." Gray was to her "like a soft shawl around the shoulders." Yellow was "like the sun. It means life and is rich in promise." She knew two kinds of brown. One was "warm and friendly like leaf mold." The other was "like the trunks of aged trees with wormholes, or like withered hands."

Houses were layers of life aromatic with their histories. She recognized an old-fashioned country house because "it has several layers of odors left by a succession of families, of plants, of perfumes, and draperies." Smell also told her about people she met. "In the odor of young men," she said, "there is something elemental, as of fire, storm, and salt sea. It pulsates with buoyancy and desire."

Asked what she knew about cities, she painted a vivid sensory portrait. "Long streets. Tramping feet, smells from windows, tobacco, pipes, gas, fruits, aromas, tiers upon tiers of odor. Automobiles. A whir that make me shiver, a rumble."

Who was this woman of multiple senses? Her name was Helen Keller, and when I was eight I had the rare privilege of talking to her while she read my lips with her hand. "Why are you so happy?" I blurted with a child's brutal honesty. My question amused her, and she replied in her odd and mysterious voice, "It is because I live each day as if it were my last. And life, in all its moments, is so filled with glory."

Was Helen Keller disabled? Technically, yes. Essentially, no. She had rewoven the filaments of the senses that remained to her into a net that could catch the world and its creatures. She knew them with an intimacy and accuracy that made her life glorious. With such glory she was impassioned to reach out to the deaf and blind, to minorities and the poor. Her sensitivity to justice and social need were acute, perhaps rendered more so by her new-won senses.

In some ways, we are all Helen Keller. Few of us have escaped serious crippling. We have had our senses shuttered, blinkered, closed down. We have been taught to value concepts over percepts, abstractions over the fecundity of direct sensory knowledge. Unlike Helen Keller, most of us accept our limitations and live out lives much less juicy, much less useful, than they can be.

Can we, like Helen, transcend our disabilities, heal the betrayal of our sensory life? Can we, like Helen, go deeper into that vast storehouse of alternative ways of knowing and bring back new ways of savoring the richness and glory of the physical world? Can we, like Helen, be inspired by our senses to feel the world's problems so powerfully that we are moved to take action to solve them?

There is no question that our primary knowledge of the world comes through sensory and physical experience. In childhood our senses are acute—how green the grass, how velvety cold and sweet the ice cream, how ticklish a bare-foot run through the meadow. Wordsworth's great poem "Intimations of Immortality in Early Childhood" celebrates the sensory brilliance of childhood:

There was a time when meadow, grove and stream,
the earth and every common sight,
To me did seem
Apparelled in celestial light,
The glory and the freshness of a dream. . . .

When we grow up, Wordsworth laments, the freshness and divinity of the world are hidden from our direct perception, and "nothing can bring back the hour of splendor in the grass, of glory in the flower."

Yet embraced in another way, maturity can mean that our capacity for a glorious celebration of our senses is even greater. Adulthood brings with it the potential to appreciate erotic love and aesthetic joy, a sense of shadows to heighten the sunlight, passion, paradox, contemplative intelligence—the whole human comedy and tragedy.

To regain full use of the senses in adulthood requires some effort on our part, but the labor is filled with delights. How many of us would balk at being asked to taste, touch, smell, see, and feel as many wonderful things as possible?

Moreover, we can approach our task with the knowledge that as we wake up our senses, we activate our capacity to think, feel, and understand things in multiple ways. We enrich our concepts and lay down new pathways to appreciating the world about us and within us.

Let me demonstrate what I mean. Look around the place you are sitting in now, and make note of some object. It can be anything, small or large, familiar or strange—a potted plant on the window sill, a painting on the wall, a child's toy, the house across the road, the pattern on the ceiling. We will come back to this object in a moment.

Now as you read, allow yourself to imagine as vividly as you can these sensory experiences:

* Wriggling your toes in hot sand and listening to the lapping rhythm of ocean waves.

* The taste of fresh apricots.

* The smell of freshly baked bread.

* A tender good-night kiss.

* The sound of galloping horses.

* Rolling in a pile of freshly fallen autumn leaves.

* Standing at night outside a church in a soft snowfall listening to a choir rehearsing the *Messiah*.

* Holding hands at the movies.

* Having your cheek nuzzled and licked by a puppy.

Now take a moment to close your eyes and remember other favorite physical pleasures, bringing the sensations back as if you are experiencing them again right now. . . .

When you open your eyes, look again at the object you had noted before. What do you notice about its color? Its shape? The way it catches the light? Your sense of its depth and weight? The very memory of things we have delighted in can activate sensory acuity.

Remember our journey to the four levels of self in the previous chapter? Now we are going deeper into the sensory realm, with our consciousness fully engaged in every delicious sensation. Your visit will be most beneficial if you use your sensory memory to imagine as vividly as you can the experiences I suggest. Doing so strengthens the muscles of your inner imaginative senses.

The most consistently creative people I know have given much time and thought to developing their inner senses. The anthropologist Margaret Mead regularly entered her interior realms to explore issues she was working on. She

43

once described to me the process she used to write an important speech on the humanitarian uses of science.

She began by visualizing an art exhibit she had seen in Copenhagen in which the human body was made to look grotesque. This reminded her of scientific studies she had read that reduced the human condition to graphs and statistics. Then she pictured her audience of scientists and saw them as shut down to art and music, eyes veiled, ears stopped up. Suddenly she was filled with the swelling sounds of Beethoven and found herself gazing up at the glorious figures on the ceiling of the Sistine Chapel. Finally she recalled the face of a New Guinean friend, "primitive" in 1928, an intellectual sophisticate in 1953.

Images joined images, words began to form, and a complex and potent speech unfolded. If an exacting scientist like Margaret Mead could use inner imagery and memory to spur creative thinking, we can surely train ourselves to do the same, whatever our interests or concerns.

As we prepare now to enter into the inner sensory realm, it would be helpful for you to gather five objects related to the five senses. As I write, I have a cat nearby to touch, a Native American wool painting to see, crickets to hear, a potpourri of dried lemons, oranges, and limes to smell, and a banana to taste. Take a moment to get your sensory materials together, and then we'll begin.

Ready? We start as we did before by traveling up and around the mountain of self, smelling the pine trees, feeling the crunch of leaves and pine needles under our feet. Birds are singing, and the wind is soughing in the trees. Blue sky and dappling sunlight break through openings in the tree-tops.

Repeating the same pattern of imaginative experiences each time we wish to enter the inner realms gives our minds a kind of map to follow that with practice can be used to travel quickly to our interior spaces.

Once again, then, you reach the top of the mountain and raise the great stone tablet that covers the inner passageway. Once again you descend the darkened stairway, down and around the spiral path into the mountain's interior.

There's the first door ahead, the door to the Realm of the Senses. You can already smell it. Carnations and hot cinnamon buns. What does it smell like to you today?

The door has changed since you last visited. Your sensory palate has already become richer and more varied. A gossamer silvery spider's web brushes your cheek, droplets of dew attached to the strands, each tiny globe sparkling and perfectly defined. A sun-warm, downy peach luscious with juices is waiting to be tasted, and the intricate counterpoint of a Mozart concerto is dancing in your ears. In fact, Mozart himself is winking at you from one of the panels, a small man in a ruffled yellow silk suit and elaborate white wig, playing the pianoforte.

Pulling open the heavy door, you enter a darkened and silent space. A woman's hand reaches out to touch yours. Her fingers tap a greeting into your palm, her fingers caressing your hand like welcoming green leaves.

It is Helen Keller, and she is inviting you to accompany her to a place where the tactile senses reign. Her fingertips transmit a charge, an enhancement of your own sensitivity to texture. With a gentle motion, she indicates that you should sit and hold out your hands to receive the universe of touch. After each sensation of touch, imagine that you shake your hands and they instantly become clean, fresh, and ready for the next sensation.

Here is silk like molten water. Holding it is like catching clouds.

Here is a purring cat, kneading happy paws on your knees.

Here is cashmere like a hug from your mother.

Here, folded around you, is an eiderdown quilt, a lofting of feathers embraced in cotton.

Enjoy the sticky viscous feeling of pulling taffy.

Caress the long soft nose of a horse.

Feel a stone rubbed to cool smoothness by a flowing brook.

Helen leads you now to her favorite oak tree. Embracing the bark, you know the sensations of time captured and of wisdom held in your hands.

Helen now places a single rose petal in your hand. Its fragile delicate energy is supple and soft, like a baby's kiss.

Now your hands are plunged into a barrel of potato chips. They are crackling and paper thin, with grains of salt clinging to their greasy concave surfaces. Your hands go mad for a minute and crush as many chips as they can.

Now warm sticky honey is being poured slowly over your hands. At the same time, an ice cube is placed on the back of your neck. Try to feel them both at the same time.

Now, in the darkness, many come forward to shake your hand. A child places her hand in yours. Now the hand of a shy adolescent. Now a large dog extends a paw. Now the hand that shakes yours belongs to a man trying to sell you a car. Now it's a woman applying for a job. Now the hand of a political candidate. Now the hand of a gardener. Now receive in yours the weathered but strong hand of your grandfather.

As a final gift, Helen places in your hand a large lump of clay. Her fingers on yours indicate that she wants you to shape it into a model of your own hands. You experience the mystery of hands making hands, a godlike act, creation at its most basic.

In the hands that you sculpt are memories of things you've touched and been touched by. For touching is not simply a physical act; it carries ideas and feelings also. Each sense perception is also a sensibility, and our hearts can be touched as well as our hands.

With your sensitivity to touch now so activated, reflect for a moment on the wonder of what you've been doing. The skin we so take for granted is the body's largest organ, a space suit for our earthbound existence. Its billions of nerve endings make up our most primitive sense.

Touch is said to be ten times more potent than verbal or emotional contact. Hands lift us out of the womb, guide and caress us on our paths through life, and carry us into our

47

graves. Babies need touch and holding to thrive and grow. Rocked and cuddled, they become alert and responsive and develop the capacity for physical and emotional pleasure.

As adults as well, our abilities are enhanced by a heightened sense of touch. Develop touch, and you become more responsive to all the prickling, tingling, fondling forces that make up our palette of feelings. Develop touch, and you gain sensitivity to the emotional "textures" of life.

Touch teaches us to distinguish between smooth people and abrasive ones. It helps us hang in there when rough patches dominate our emotional landscape, and it invites us not to take silken times for granted.

A high-touch mother I know helps her children cope with emotional bruising by encouraging them to use touch words to describe their interactions. As they cut and paste scraps of fabrics, mold clay, and build constructions of rocks and sand, they talk about how the rough edges of a troublesome classmate might be smoothed or the sharp style of a teacher made bearable. As a team builder in corporate life, she uses much the same technique with middle management!

Regular practice in high touch forges connections between your aesthetic capacities and your touch receptors. Soon you will be tactilely brilliant! Let me offer some suggestions:

⁎ Take some time to enter consciously into the touches of the seasons. Walk in a garden in the springtime. Let your fingers gently squeeze the swelling flower buds, be tickled by the fuzzy cattails, uncurl the fern fronds. Lie on your back and feel the sun warming your face.

* Be adventurous in the fruit and vegetable section of your grocery. Touch the delicate skins and grainy rinds of the bounty that has seeded and budded and fruited in the fields and orchards of Israel and Chile and California for your tactile appreciation. Give them poetic epithets—wanton peach, maidenly apricot, sulky turnip, passionate plum. Words help anchor your sensations and keep them coming.

* Clothing stores are marvelous places to continue your tactile education. Visit your favorite to touch the tweeds, embrace the brocades, shimmy into the silks, and meet the starched cotton on its own terms.

49

With so much high tech around us, we need much more high touch for balance. So reach out now to the highly touchable thing you selected for this session. As you touch your object, see if you can experience it in a new way, as if it were trying to offer you tactile pleasure. Its surfaces rise up to meet your hand, just as you are cradling it.

I've picked up my kitten and am greatly enjoying stroking his sinuous body. As he arches his back in ecstasy, I find I am purring as well.

From touch, let's move now to another sense linked with basic pleasures. I once met a man whose whole life seemed to be built on the theme of "yum, yum, yum." He was the great gourmand and food writer James Beard.

A jolly, ample man, Beard had an enormous capacity for pleasure. To watch him smell roses was to understand roses. Observing him eat roast pork, juices dribbling down his chin, meant seeing enjoyment that was positively Shakespearean. He had one of the most complete memories for tastes of anyone who has ever lived, and he could reconstruct in gustatory memory the details of every good meal he had eaten.

My aunt Annette worked in the office of the heart doctor whom Beard consulted. "I'm not about to die for a long, long time," he told my aunt. "I'm enjoying myself too much." Gusto must be therapeutic, for true to his word, Beard savored life until the ripe age of eighty-two. A true inhabitant of the Realm of the Senses, he will certainly be here.

Yes, there he is, wearing a chef's white apron, his cherubic face gleaming like a grown-up baby's as he invites you to taste the dishes he has prepared, set out on a dazzling white linen cloth.

Taste any delectable thing you wish from this banquet for one. Let the morsels roll in your mouth. Along with taste and texture, savor the food's color and form, its stored energy and light. Food is ultimately sun sent, Sol's endless gift. Read the foods he offers not merely as a menu but as a feast for the senses, to feed and grow the imagination.

Let's begin with the appetizers. First, tender baby artichoke hearts, marinated in olive oil, lemon, and garlic, with hints of thyme, oregano, and marjoram. Now try tiny puffs of pastry stuffed with crabmeat and capers. Enhanced by the sea-bright flavor of the crab, the capers explode in your mouth, at once tangy and peppery. Here are freshly made tortilla chips to scoop up emerald guacamole, silky mashed avocado with undertones of garlic and cilantro.

Taste now a trio of breads fresh from the oven. Floury mounds of savory sourdough. Golden braided challah, yellow with eggs and laced with raisins. Whole-grain loaves crunchy with seed-studded crusts.

What other kinds of bread do you remember? Bread is the staff of life, and slathered with butter, dipped in oil, or smeared with jam, it fires our thoughts as it builds our bones. Is it any wonder that the gods and goddesses of grains were among the most venerated in ancient pantheons?

A salad of field greens awaits your pleasure, mesclun, arugula, watercress, endive, leaves that bite you back, chastened by a simple dressing of virgin olive oil and balsamic vinegar.

Try some of the main dishes now. Here's grilled fillet of salmon, crispy on the outside and flaky pink within. Or choose deep-dish chicken pot pie. Chunks of white meat swimming in cream sauce with cubes of potato, carrot rounds, and mushrooms buried like treasures under a buttery crust. Your fork pierces, and aromatic steam that is the essence of chicken rises to salute your nose.

At the head of the table Beard is carving a massive prime rib of beef, rare or medium as you wish. A medley of vegetables completes the platter, potatoes mashed with

51

cream and butter, delicate spears of spring-fresh asparagus, mushrooms redolent with earth magic and the mystery of the woods.

What favorite dishes from memory would you like to taste again? Did your mother spend hours simmering rich chicken soup? Or your fisherman father bring home baskets of trout to flour and fry? What do you cook when you feel like celebrating? What treat brings comfort when you're feeling blue? Taste them now.

I hope you saved room for dessert. Beard is laying out a personal favorite—dark chocolate mousse with whipped cream and a spangling of crystallized violets. Or perhaps a crisp tart, apple slices layered like waves and topped with rich caramel. Or a coconut cake, moist and shimmering like a mound of fresh fallen snow.

Top off your meal with everyone's favorite. Ice cream sundaes of every kind. Which will it be—French vanilla, dark chocolate, strawberry, peppermint, pistachio, or your favorite flavor? There are toppings, too—hot fudge, butterscotch, blueberry, marshmallow fluff, whipped cream, chopped nuts, candy sparkles, maraschino cherries. Layer it all up in an crystal sundae glass, and dig in with a silvery long-handled spoon.

What a blessing that something so enjoyable as tasting wonderful foods is good for us as well! But so it is. An enhanced palate is one of the keys to a life that savors the varied joys of living.

Taste teaches us to seek out the yummy in art and music, friends and ideas. It heightens our appreciation for the sweet, sour, pungent, spicy flavors of life's rich repast. It motivates us to stir the pot of experience and add new and exotic ingredients. A savorer is a creator, an artist at the feast of life's table. Pity poor fools who limit themselves to a mass-produced, white-bread existence.

The elegant French writer Marcel Proust was inspired to write *Remembrance of Things Past* by nibbling on a madeleine cookie. One taste of this childhood favorite brought on a torrent of memories, which culminated in a masterpiece.

For us, too, foods are memory bound. The many tastes of our lives have stories attached, along with emotions. For me, spinach triggers a sense of strength and well-being. As a child I always linked the muscle-bound vigor of Popeye with eating that leafy green. Plowing through a steaming dish of lasagna, I am entirely Sicilian. Its flavorful layers conjure up endless childhood meals with my Mediterranean relatives.

What foods bring back the remembrance of events and people of your past? What bean or berry, fish or fowl, cake or custard, more than just food, is your past on a platter?

Here are some other ways to venture into the temple of taste:

* Visit a cheese store or deli that offers an array of unusual choices. Try some aged cheese, for in cheese as in life, aging brings out the flavor and richness of existence. Sample a blue-veined and spicy Gorgon-

zola, a great runny Camembert, a buttery Brie. Or try several varieties of olives—green, brown, black, purple, fat with oil, wrinkled with hot peppers and herbs.

* Dine out with friends at an unfamiliar ethnic restaurant, savoring the delights of a new cuisine. Become a multicultural eater, and you will find that your mind and thought will expand as well.

* Eat a simple meal in silence, with Zenlike attention to the color, texture, aroma, temperature, and taste of every spoon and forkful. Make the meal a mindfulness meditation, gently bringing your wandering thoughts back to the actions and sensations of each present moment.

* Bake bread, reflecting at each step on what you are doing and how it relates to your life: sifting, stirring, yeasting, kneading, baking. By the time you get around to eating, you have a whole philosophy!

* Read cookbooks or food magazines and try to taste in your mind the recipes you are reading. Then make the dish and see how close your imagined tastes were to the real thing.

* Exotic fruit has a way of bringing out the tropics in our souls. So buy and taste a variety—star fruit and papaya, mangoes and ripe pineapples—whatever your market has.

* Every so often gather your friends to make a meal around a theme: Love. Elegance. Simplicity. Ecstasy. Awakening. And see what miracles happen.

Take up the object you gathered for tasting, and taste it now. Let its flavors and textures announce themselves in different parts of your mouth. Sweet at the tip of the tongue, bitter at the back, sour at the sides, and salty everywhere. Suggest to yourself that from this moment your sense of taste will be heightened.

Ready to see something new? Here is our guide to the world of vision, the great American artist Georgia O'Keeffe. A lady of the elements, her pioneer face stark and eagle-eyed, she looks like one of her own New Mexico desert landscapes.

55

She asks you first to gaze with her at the immensity of the New Mexico sky. In the desert, she says, light is elemental. Do you see how the distant hills make a natural canvas for a palette of color shifting from black to dark brown to blue, rust, and blazing gold? Imagine the joy of an artist who lives in a landscape where singing skies and radiant cliffs paint themselves anew each hour as the light changes.

Everywhere there is form and pattern. Shapes and colors repeat in large and small details. In the middle distance, rocks tumble together in chaos and perfect beauty. Beneath your feet, the pebbly sand echoes their design in miniature. Nearby a spiny green cactus and bleached white cow skull pair in a natural still life, as do the white adobe church and black wooden cross silhouetted against the horizon.

Like English artist and poet William Blake, O'Keeffe knows little difference between the artist and the mystic. She, too, asks us to see "infinity in a grain of sand and heaven in a wild flower."

Suddenly O'Keeffe's mood changes, and with it the locale. You are with her in an airplane flying east to where she began her career. Look down at the changing contours as you sail over the Rockies and the Great Plains. A quilt of farmer's fields, edged with wooded windbreaks and dotted with red barns and white houses, spreads out beneath you.

As darkness comes you fly over a city and its carpet of lights. The plane banks, and the buildings rush up to meet you, then disappear into flatness and a gray landing strip.

The city is an austere world of steel and glass, grids, angles, geometry. You wonder about the lives behind all those windows. O'Keeffe directs your gaze down to the pavement. Shoes of all descriptions scurry past—loafers, sandals, cross-trainers, English broughams, high-heeled pumps, hiking boots, hightop sneakers—attached to lives whose joys and griefs you will never know.

Leaving the city, you travel by train to a place of trees and lakes. As you walk through the forest, O'Keeffe shares with you her fascination for the very small. Look closely, she suggests, at a fallen tree and see the tiny universes it houses, green-gray moss forests and mushroom cities, sap droplets like jewel lakes, busy colonies of ants.

At the edge of the woods stands a brown clapboard house with a sagging splintery porch and rusty porch swing. You climb a ladder into the attic. Clothes from another age spill from dusty trunks, dresses of fading green taffeta, high-button shoes, collars and cuffs of yellowed lace.

As you stare at the jumble of broken furniture and abandoned toys, leather-bound books and bundled newspapers, you see in your mind's eye your own attic or closet. What treasures of your past are there? One by one you call up their images, their color, their shape, the memories and feelings they trigger.

As you prepare to leave, O'Keeffe, the priestess of still life, hands you a few of her favorites. Here is a spiraling snail shell, whorls of pink and gray opalescence. Here a ram's horn, a voluptuous apple, a weathered fence rail.

57

Last, she hands you an iris. You see it now as she does, a secret universe. Its shapes and hollows expand and reverberate in your mind until they are more than themselves and become almost human, female, reproductive. "When you take a flower in your hand," she says, "it's your world for the moment. I want to give you that world. I want you to know that looking is engaging the soul."

Perhaps the reason looking engages the soul is that seeing engages a great deal of the brain. Seventy percent of our sense receptors are located in the eyes. It is no wonder, then, that seeing is the principal way we appraise and comprehend the world.

But actual seeing with the eyes and the brain is only part of the picture. The way we choose to frame reality with our inward eyes sets in play a whole range of creative and emotional forces.

"I see what you are saying," we tell our friend, mixing metaphors to persuade her of our sympathy.

A little light bulb goes off in our head, and we have a sudden flash of comprehension—an "in-sight."

How we process the information of both physical and inner seeing—how we frame it, shape it, reimagine it—often determines how our life will proceed. "Seeing is believing," we are told, but we could just as easily say, "Believing is seeing."

I know a brother-and-sister pair of fraternal twins who see the world quite differently. They may look at the same event, but while he tends to see only things that are wrong and headed for disaster, she sees wonder and beauty and how everything may work out to great benefit. Understandably, their lives diverge when it comes to "luck" and opportunity. "My life is cursed," he often says, while she believes, "My life is blessed."

Sight is also "vision." Visionaries are people who see patterns of possibilities before they emerge in time or who grasp easily the overall nature of things. It is fascinating to discover how many of these geniuses of in-sight also have a highly developed physical sense of sight.

The great mystic Hildegard of Bingen could describe a leaf with the same diligence with which she could detail the Divine Reality behind reality. Her botanical descriptions were as vivid and complex as her revelations of the greening powers of God.

Would you like to be a visionary? Let Mother Nature help you. Find a wonderful tree. Look closely at the patterns in its bark, and describe them as vividly as you can, in speech or writing.

Then take an idea or problem that concerns you and look again at the bark, this time allowing the patterns you see to reveal their insights into your problem.

Finally, if you wish, focus on a philosophical or spiritual issue or global problem. Looking once more, see how the bark enlightens your mind with its "answers."

We think of the eyes as windows to the soul. This quality of translucence has always linked the eyes to spiritual reality. In some faiths, deep seeing is a kind of worship. Hindu devotees are constantly traveling across India seeking a spiritual charge in the visual communion called darshan, in which the teacher beholds the student with a silent, penetrating gaze.

If you would like to experience the wonder of such deep seeing for yourself, here's a way to proceed. Choose a trusted friend with whom to practice. Take each other's hands, close your eyes, and tell each other that when you open your eyes again, you will see not just the other's external appearance but also the inner beauty that shines from each of you. Then open your eyes and receive with your eyes the depth of soul that each human being contains.

Seeing can heal our bodies as well as our souls. The correlation between imagery and healing has been well documented. But what is most interesting is how a change in the images you hold about your body can result in a change in health. Positive imagery can work as a force of nature, helping the body to restore itself to its more optimal condition. Negative or toxic imagery does the opposite.

Ask yourself, are you holding a death wish or a life wish about your existence? You would be surprised how many people get into a loop of chronic self-destructive thinking, sending out a regular stream of image signals that tell their bodies to sicken.

You are more in charge of your health and well-being than you ever imagined. This is the terrible or wonderful freedom that comes with being human. So try to catch yourself whenever you are in a self-destruct mode and say, "STOP!" Then consciously change the images you are holding about yourself. Soon your mood will change as well, along with your sense of life's possibilities.

Try also to spend a few minutes each day holding a picture of your body and your mind in a state of splendid health. Become very familiar with the image. You may be surprised and gratified by the improvements that result.

As if this weren't enough reason to develop your powers of sight, vision is also linked to the creative imagination. The greatest store in the world is not on Fifth Avenue or Rodeo Drive or the Champs Élysées. It is in your own brain, and its shelves display a cornucopia of images ready to be joined with other images into new ideas, perceptions, even stories.

Visual thinking allows us to see a project or idea as a whole. When we think logically or verbally about a problem, our inner process tends to go 1–2–3–4–5 or A-B-C-D-E, but people who develop their capacity for inner imagery can picture a project from start to finish in an instant. The visual brain is capable of processing millions of images in microseconds and giving us a "read-out" packed into a few information-filled symbols or images.

Creative minds are generally engaged in imagistic thinking, racing over alternatives, picking, choosing, discarding, synthesizing, sometimes doing the work of several months in a few minutes.

In my research I have often found that people who solve problems by working with their inner imagery tend to complete their project more often and more easily.

Why? Because thinking in images creates fire in the mind, visions in the soul, and energy in the body. It helps you not only finish the project but do so in a way that fits comfortably into the patterns of your inner universe.

A well-known novelist who is a friend of mine writes as well as he does by closing his eyes and watching the story as it unfolds in images. "Then I just put it down on paper," he explains. "I tell my mind, I want a story. And my mind says, okay, here it is. Just watch."

Imagery, then, provides an environment as real and as influential as the tangible environment of our outward life. Seeing is a creative act in which we have enormous freedom, should we decide to take it, to re-vision our world.

Think of what needs changing in your world. Ask your image-making mind to help you, close your eyes, and let the

61

story roll! At first, you may get only random images that seem disconnected, but as you keep asking the question, gradually the images will become more coherent, useful, and creative.

You may even come to wonder, "Who is putting on this great show for me? I couldn't have thought of that in a hundred years!" But Something in you did and will continue to do so if you use the codes of inner imagery.

With all this in mind, let us look creatively at the object we chose to explore through sight. Examine carefully its shape and size, the details of its structure. Consider its colors and the moods they evoke in you. Switch places and imagine that you are the object looking back at yourself. Then, once again, look at the object in the usual way.

Note what has happened to your seeing. Chances are that colors are richer and more varied, form has taken on greater depth, the play of light and shadow is both more present and more subtle. And, if you close your eyes, you probably can recreate the object with your inner vision.

By committing yourself to an enhanced inner visual life, not only will you expand the joys of seeing, you may even improve your physical eyesight.

Here are some ways to keep developing your visionary powers:

* Spend some time each day just looking at things. As Georgia O'Keeffe said, "In a way, nobody sees a flower really, it is so small, we haven't time—and to see takes time, like to have a friend takes time."

* Look for O'Keeffe paintings in your local art museum or library. Spend some time as well with the Impressionists—Monet, Renoir, Cezanne—French geniuses of light. Then visit a photograph gallery to see how nature is captured through the eye of the camera. Ansel Adams's and Galen Rowell's photographs will help you see mountain landscapes in fresh ways.

* Visualize with your inner eye a place that is nearby and familiar. Put in as many specific details as you can. Then go and look at the place and see how accurately you pictured it. Close your eyes and use your visual imagination to add new features to your inner picture.

* Place a flower in a vase and observe as many details as you can. Then sketch the flower, working in the details you have observed. Now close your eyes and imagine that you can enter the flower and discover the world within. Allow your imagination to evolve into a story about that world.

* Taking this further, each day give yourself an image and allow your mind to "story" it. You might imagine that you are walking down a city street and an alligator comes waddling toward you. What happens next in your imaginative world? Then take any event or idea that concerns you, place it in an image that you can relate to, and watch as your novelistic mind goes

to work and unfolds solutions as a story or a series of images.

* Practice deep seeing with friends and family (especially children), and then share with each other how it feels to be so seen.

Who will guide us through the world of smells? Don't laugh, but it's that hammy movie star Babe the Pig who has a tremendous nose for all kinds of smells. Let's follow along as he ambles in his random, piggy way from one interesting odor to another.

First he takes us outside to revel in the smell of the earth after a rain. It's a soul-satisfying smell that takes us, quite literally, to our roots. Next, he leads us into a pine forest where we enjoy the crisp greeny smell of the tall trees.

Now we are in a garden fragrant with the opulent smell of roses. Bend down and inhale the sweet spice of carnations. There's bed of lavender, and don't miss the lush tropical aromas emanating from the gardenia bush. Babe wanders happily along, and we follow him to drench ourselves in the fragrance of a blossoming orange grove.

A country home is Babe's next stop. The horses in the field next to the house exude a warm musky smell. Even their fresh droppings are strangely pleasant to the nose. In the backyard we catch the clean scent of freshly washed sheets flapping in the sun.

Babe leads us to the kitchen door. Entering, we are met with a wonderful array of cooking smells—brewing coffee, bread baking, hot gingerbread, cloves simmering in apple cider, even chicken soup bubbling on the stove.

Trotting after Babe into the living room, we relax into the pungent, smoky scent of wood burning in the fireplace. Uh-oh. Babe's snuffling has located a box of chocolates melting in the heat. We can't resist, either. We'd better leave before Babe gets us into trouble.

Babe has a mischievous idea, and before long we are investigating a number of ethnic restaurants with their unmistakable, complex smells. The soy and sesame oil perfume of a Chinese restaurant. The familiar cheese and tomato sauce richness of a pizza parlor. The briny, ocean smell of an oyster bar. The bright tangy smell of peppers and salsa in the Southwestern cantina.

Babe now performs a little magic and leads you to visit the smells that take you back to childhood. Buttered popcorn at the movies. A puppy's breath. Chalk dust. The inside of your family's new car. Pipe smoke. The powerful smell of diesel trains. The melting tar of a macadam road.

Think now of smells from your early life, and Babe will bring you to them. With them will come other smells, other memories. . . .

Each season has a smell, and Babe knows them all. You are led to enjoy the damp warm smell of spring when trees begin to go green. The freshly mown grass of summer. The smoky sharpness of burning leaves in autumn. The winter warmth of chestnuts roasting.

For his finale, Babe takes you to a circus where strange odors mix with more familiar sawdust and peanuts. The furry odor of caged tigers. The fire swallower reeking of smoke and gasoline. Are you surprised at how sweet an elephant smells? Or exhilarated by the smell of fear in a crowd as it watches the tightrope walker?

Babe has his own circus favorite. He sniffs appreciatively at the cloying sweetness of a pink pillow of cotton candy, dives in, and disappears.

Smell is primitive and powerful, but it is also subtle and evocative. It gives us clues to our safety as well as our seductions. When you follow your nose, you are apt to end up in a lot of interesting places—barbecues, beaches, old bookstores, the arms of a beloved. When you follow your nose, you sniff out the aromatics of existence, know when to advance or retreat, leap into adventure or run for your life.

Did you know that you are able to discern over ten thousand different odors? And a good thing, too, in a world where smoking wires, leaking gas tanks, and faulty refrigeration offers too many industrial doors to our permanent departure from this life.

But our noses are nothing when it comes to our four-footed friends. Babe the Pig may have a connoisseur's nose, but his cousin Minnette in the Perigord region of France makes him look positively anosmic, which means, of course, "without smell."

Minnette is a truffle sow, and she will passionately pursue and dig up those incredibly expensive and sensual fungi even though they lie under six inches of soil.

Why? Because to Minnette, truffles smell curiously like a sexy boar. Perhaps that's not so odd. How many women

66

of your acquaintance spend huge sums on perfumes and lotions to pursue a sexy bore?

And then there are dogs. I have an ancient dog who is well over a hundred years old in dog terms. His hearing isn't much, and his sight is fading, but his nose is ever young.

The other day I followed him as he smelled his rickety but certain way through the neighborhood. Every street was for him an olfactory civilization—a museum of old rubbish here, a hospital of old bones there, past history and the day's news written on the curbs and trees by dogs who left something of themselves behind.

"Hi, Barnaby, and any other dogs that amble by," the message written in scent seems to say. "This is Poopsie, the spaniel. I just ate some meat scraps from the garbage of the restaurant down the block. Come find me, and we'll try for more."

And there goes Barnaby, tracking the molecules of Poopsie's paws like the bloodhound he's not. Soon he finds Poopsie, and they sniff each other appreciatively and join noses for further olfactory adventures.

I sigh in envy and return home. What's Barnaby got that I have not?

About forty-four times more scent receptors. My ancestors, unlike Barnaby's, lifted their noses up off the ground and in the process lost several hundred million receptors. But we humans are left with enough, some five million, to receive our scent-rich world.

How many odors can you detect right now in the room where you are reading? Walk around, sniff out your closet,

67

your shoes, the rug, the residue of cleaning products, flowers, plants, other people or animals, and even yourself. Open drawers and take good sniff. Close them and see if the odors remain. Do any of them bring an uprush of memories?

Memory is tied to smell. I, for one, cannot smell "Evening in Paris" perfume without hurling back in time to relive the agonies of my first date.

Open the window and breathe in the varieties of odors that rush in to supplant those of the room.

Years ago my dad, a comedy writer, used to write jokes for Jimmy Durante, a whimsical gent with a prominent beak. "Da nose knows," he would proclaim while tapping his most famous feature. And he was right!

Every sniff brings the world through your nose. It has been estimated that in any given three-week period, some molecules of everyone on this planet pass through your breathing apparatus—your aunt Annie, the president of France, a giraffe in Kenya. Imagine the amount of information you are downloading through your nose from the atmosphere.

In fact, the atmosphere is what your breath is all about. Inhale, and you nourish your body and mind with the oxygen it needs to keep you going; exhale, and you release the carbon dioxide that the plants need to keep them going.

Focus on your breath, following it all the way in and all the way out a hundred times or so, and your very consciousness changes.

Conscious breathing is key to all the meditation systems of the world. Yoga, tai chi, zazen, and other Eastern prac-

68

tices use breathing as the basis for their disciplines. Conscious breathing relaxes you, releases stress, restores balance in your body, quiets and deepens your mind, and even brings you to the Source of your existence.

So take the next few minutes and focus only on your breathing, the long intake and the long release. Think of nothing but your breathing and the awareness that you are becoming the very atmosphere. Soon your consciousness will be as translucent as the air around you. Or it will become so, if you continue this practice.

Would you now please bring to your nose whatever it is that you have chosen to smell. I have just inhaled the potpourri and find myself awash in scent—old roses, dried orange peels, pine cones, lavender. More than merely interesting, now that my sense of smell is activated, the fragrances inhabit my head and become a part of me.

As I write these words, Barnaby has just come in from one of his olfactory jaunts, wet from the rain. Instead of wrinkling my nose in disgust, I breathe deeply of the damp, furry warmth arising from his thick Akita coat.

Now it's your turn. Notice what has happened to your olfactory sense—the very shape and presence, the personality even of what you are smelling. It's different now, isn't it?

If you wish to have this heightened aromatic capacity, through activities like those I have suggested, your sense of smell can be enhanced.

Here are a few things you can do to continue to educate your nose:

69

* Explore the contents of your kitchen cabinets with your nose. Savor the extracts, spices, and flavorings. Let them tell your their story. Try to call up in your mind the lands they came from just from their smells.

* Go to a store's perfume counter and try to distinguish among the various scents offered for testing. Notice especially the differences between colognes offered for men and for women.

* Try burning various kinds of incense. Incense has been burned for millennia to lure the noses of the gods so that they might return and set our world to rights. Note what happens to the general atmosphere of your home when incense is burned.

70

* Read the Song of Songs in the Bible and try to smell in your imagination the array of aromatics offered there.

* Sniff something that was important to you as a child, a kind of food, perhaps, and observe how many memories rise up.

* Tomorrow morning, become mindful of the many smells that greet your morning rituals: toothpaste, soap, shampoo, coffee, tea, toast, the morning paper, and so forth.

* Note and catalog the different smells that accompany your daily routine: office smells, car aromas, visits to other homes or places, dinner smells, the odors of daytime and nighttime.

Our ears are pricked by the sound of a piano being played with elegance and gusto. We follow the sound and find that it's Mozart himself at the keyboard. With a brilliant flourish of ascending scales and a resounding final chord, he rises merrily to greet us.

We follow the clip, clip of his high-heeled shoes down a gleaming stone corridor and enter a large drawing room where an orchestra is poised to play for us.

One by one the instruments raise their particular voices. We hear the brassy ta-ta of the trumpet, the piercing sweetness of the flute, the mellow warmth of the cello, the emotional vibrato of the violin, the beat of the drum, the angelic cascades of the harp, the sensuous shivery notes of the oboe.

Mozart raises his arms to conduct, and each instrument joins in to create *Eine Kleine Nachtmusik* ("A Little Night Music"). How wondrous that so much glory could come from the trembling of molecules of air!

Mozart explains that when he composes, he first hears the music inside his head, then he writes it down. He invites you to listen to the music inside yourself.

Try it now and discover what music you hear when you close your eyes. Listen for the songs or styles that are your special favorites. My eyes get misty whenever I hear the old English tune "Greensleeves," and I thrill to the boisterous exuberance of Broadway show tunes.

Perhaps you have a special fondness for an old Beatles song, the down-home lilt of new country music, or the

71

theme from a special movie. Take a moment to close your eyes and listen to your most-loved music now. . . .

Mozart finds our modern music very funny and begins to laugh. Suddenly there is laughter everywhere. Gurgling babies, the high-pitched squeals of rambunctious children, teenaged girls giggling. Hoots and snickers, chuckles and titters, beery guffaws and raucous howls enfold you in waves of merriment.

Still laughing, Mozart leads us out into the streets of eighteenth-century Vienna. Its world of sound is quite different from our city streets. Vendors of every sort push carts over the cobblestones crying out their wares: "Fish, fresh fish!" "Peaches. Who will buy my juicy ripe peaches?" "Old clothes for sale."

You hear a thundering clatter as the magnificent coach of a royal personage sweeps by, accompanied by a mounted guard. Behind them come the rhythmic marching boots of a troop of king's men and the swish of women's long skirts as they brush the ground. It seems that from every open window comes the sound of someone playing an instrument. Vienna is the city of music, and everyone plays.

You turn a corner, and suddenly you are in a modern city with its quite different mechanical sounds. Mozart is astonished by the sounds of traffic, the howl of a fire engine siren, the sputter and roar of a motorcycle starting up, the whine of a jet plane overhead.

He covers his ears as you pass a man breaking cement with a jackhammer. You take him inside an office building, where he is bemused and fascinated by the ringing of a telephone, the click click click of a computer keyboard, the hum of a copying machine. "I could build my next concerto around these," he tells you.

Leaving the building, you hail a bus, which screeches as it stops for you, its engine roaring. After a short ride you get off at a park, where Mozart seems relieved to hear birdsong again. Mozart is drawn to a baseball game in progress, the crack of a bat hitting a home run and the roar of the crowd that follows.

But he is especially interested in the variety of human voices he hears in the park. Listen with him to the mother sitting on the bench reading a story to her child. A little farther away are two lovers reciting poetry to each other. Watch out for the three old men whose voices are raised in a noisy argument.

You sit down together now, and Mozart asks you to describe to him other modern sounds. Will you tell him about the clipped countdown to a space launch and the sound of the rocket rising? The sound of Martin Luther King, Jr., speaking his great invocation "I have a dream!"? The sound blips of a radio as you scan many stations. The ba-bum, ba-bum, ba-bum of a heartbeat through a doctor's stethoscope?

Together you wonder what kind of voice the universe speaks in. The chanting of Om? The hissing of the stars? Or is it the Silence that contains all sound?

As you consider this question, a band comes by practicing "When the Saints Go Marching In." Mozart jumps up in delight and joins them, banging a drum. With a wave, you bid him good-bye.

Your ears now acutely sharpened through your adventures with Mozart, you stop to reflect a moment on the mechanism of hearing. The ear seems almost the invention of some wild Rube Goldberg of a god. Consider the incredible chain of events that takes place every time we hear a sound.

Sound waves come rolling in like tides, with news from the universe pounding against the eardrum. The vibrating membrane sets in motion three tiny bones strangely named the hammer, anvil, and stirrup. The head of the hammer bone vibrates into the socket of the anvil bone, which vibrates in turn. The anvil bone moves the stirrup bone, which presses against the fluid in the inner ear. In the inner ear is a snail-shaped shell called the cochlea. Its tiny hairlike antennae sway in the waves, triggering nearby nerve cells, which send messages to the brain.

All this is necessary for us to hear crickets chirping, spaghetti boiling, Johnny whistling. All this to reveal that everything is energy, vibration, frequency, resonance. Even the most solid of material objects is ultimately a dance of constantly changing energy patterns. In its essence, reality is all rhythm, all music.

The world is sound.

When you listen deeply to another's voice, however, you hear more than just sounds. You hear as well the overtones of intention, the undertones of emotion, the melody of the speaker's soul. Every sound, every voice is the universe in miniature.

Deep listening is an art that can be learned. One begins by attending to familiar sounds—wind, rain, the purring of a cat, the clatter of pots as dinner is made, liquid pouring into a glass, the whir of the furnace or air conditioner.

Soon you begin to realize that deep listening involves the whole body. You hear not only with your ears, but also with the bones of your skull and everything linked to them. A sharp sound makes your hair stand on end. A lovely melody relaxes and smooths the tight muscles of your back.

If you would like to practice whole-body listening, try this fascinating experiment. Listen to your favorite music as if you are the instrument and the music is playing you. Soon you will understand what poet T. S. Eliot described in *The Four Quartets:*

> *music heard so deeply*
> *That it is not heard at all, but you are the music*
> *While the music lasts.*

75

Practice also listening more deeply to those around you—family, friends, business associates. Watch how your voices together make a kind of concert. As in all great music, the tones and words sounded are important, and important as well are those not sounded—the unsung melodies, the words not spoken, the silences.

Allow yourself to receive communication with all parts of your body and mind, not just with your ears. And then try to respond from heart and gut and bones and brain and, yes, even with silence.

Your voice is the vehicle of your soul's purpose. And yet the voice can sabotage our true feelings. I have a brilliant friend who is a kind of emotional genius but who speaks in such a flat monotone that what she intends to communicate falls literally on deaf ears.

To correct this, I suggested that she read poetry aloud for ten minutes each day, putting the passion and pathos she felt in the words into her tones. After several weeks of this, people began to listen to her much more engaging voice.

Remember that you are a master maker of sound. Hum the sound "Mmmmm." Then put your fingers in your ears and hum again. You will feel your head vibrate with its own music. Then, with your fingers in your ears, sing in a loud voice an uplifting song or hymn like "Amazing Grace."

Then, sing to yourself about your life, what it is now, and what you would like it to be. Make up words. Let the melody soar.

By musicking your mind, you give yourself potent sounds with which to reshape your existence.

Is this magic? Yes, but it is a kind of high science, too.

Would you now please listen to whatever it is that you have brought to this session. Close your eyes and experience the sound in every part of your body. Allow it to trigger memories and associations, colors, visual images, muscle sensations.

If it is what you wish, suggest to yourself that from this moment your sense of hearing and your ability to listen deeply will be enhanced.

Here are some other ways to hear the world more vividly:

* Listen to music of all kinds. Note each musical shape, color, and emotional tone. Listen as if the sound were emanating from somewhere deep inside you.

* Sing everywhere—in the shower, in the car, with the radio, and especially with friends. In fact, sing something right now.

* To make your voice stronger and clearer, hum at many pitches. Start by humming as low a note as you can. Then slowly hum up the scale, going as high as is comfortable.

* Read out loud to a child, a grandparent, or anyone else who will listen. Read poetry and plays, stories and novels, even newspaper and magazine articles.

* Attend a symphony concert or a musical recital in your town. Listen in turn for the unique sound of each instrument. During one piece, listen for the drums, cymbals, and other percussion instruments. During another, pay attention to the horns or the bass viols. Separate the music into its parts in your mind and then put it back together.

* Regularly sit in silence in a woods or a park or at the beach, eyes closed, just listening.

* Pray, and listen for the response.

* Sit where you are, eyes closed, and count all the sounds you can hear from this spot in five minutes. The space

heater, the sudden car honk on the street below, the drip-drip of yesterday's rain from the gutter.

Now that we've explored the five senses and considered what each can do for us, let's return to the world outside the mountain of the self and see what we've gained. Closing the door to the sensory realm, follow again the inner pathway to the top of the mountain, climb out, replace the stone tablet, and descend the outer path to your everyday world.

You might wish to put the book down now for a few minutes, stretch, and walk around a bit, even take a walk outside. Pay attention to your sense impressions. Are they sharper, brighter, more potent? Regular visits to the sensory realm either in your imagination or through the activities I have suggested will increase your perceptual abilities both within and without.

If imaginative journeys seem difficult without a voice to guide you, make a tape and guide yourself through the realm of the senses, giving yourself wonderful things to see, touch, smell, taste, and hear.

Or practice by taking a walk, eating a meal, or listening to a piece of music with mindfulness and attention. Then close your eyes and recreate the same sensory impressions in your inner world as vividly as you can.

Regular practice grows new connectors in your brain-mind system, mindgates between inner and outer reality. Once these gates are open, trade and commerce can flow between your imaginative and everyday worlds. Bridging

78

the continents of mind and body is the key to living in a larger and more vibrant reality.

Frequent visits can make you an intranaut—a fearless explorer of your inner realms. Or if computer metaphors are more to your liking, you can be intranetted, on-line with ready access to a world richer and more fascinating than your previous imaginings.

As your skill at bridging inner and outer realities increases, some very remarkable things will become possible. An enhanced imagination gives you the capacity to create the blueprint or pattern for something that you wish to actualize in the outer world.

Let me demonstrate.

Take a moment to consider something that you would like to do or create over the next year or so. Perhaps it is an artistic project. Or a new skill that you wish to acquire. It may even be a different mood or way of being or quality of life. I call this step "setting your creative intention."

Now in your imagination, picture yourself as vividly as you can in the full burst of accomplishing this intention. Perhaps you see yourself writing a book, composing a song, making new friends, getting well or getting weller, starting a new profession, or discovering new pathways in your current one. Pay special attention to the senses involved. What do you see, smell, hear, touch, and taste while doing this activity?

Then whatever your intention is, stand up and act it out, using as much of your body as is relevant to the activity. It is important that you actually move your body and enact as

79

fully as possible the successful performance of your intention. If you wish to have some stirring music accompany you during this process, by all means put some on.

Now return again to your imagination and continue to enact the intention without moving your body. Activate your inner senses more vividly this time, adding new sense impressions that occur to you. Do this for several minutes.

Then once again act out the intention physically with your whole body, imagining the sensations while your body goes through the motions. Alternate between physical and imaginary enactment several times.

When you have finished, notice how you feel about your project and intention. Is it in your bones? Can you sense it as a growing part of you? Is it more real than it was before? Did you get any new ideas about it from the storehouse of perceptions that you recently visited?

Whenever I have studied people who really get things done—people who don't give up in the middle like so many of us—I almost invariably find that they are using something like this exercise. They complete their tasks in the outer world because they are continually inspired and energized by a passion for the possible coming from the inner world. Their projects grow from inside out rather than the other way around.

Congratulate yourself! You have made a wonderful start in learning the art of manifesting your dreams. When you add the energies of the psychological, mythic, and spiritual realms to your heightened senses, your capacity for accomplishment will truly be formidable.

❦ VISITING THE PSYCHOLOGICAL REALM

It doesn't interest me what you do for a living. I want to know what you ache for, and if you dare to dream of meeting your heart's longing.

It doesn't interest me how old you are. I want to know if you will risk looking like a fool for love, for your dreams, for the adventure of being alive.

It doesn't interest me what planets are squaring your moon. I want to know if you have touched the center of your own sorrow, if you have been opened by life's betrayals or have become shriveled and closed from fear of further pain! I want to know if you can sit with pain, mine or your own, without moving to hide it or fade it or fix it. I want to know if you can be with

JOY, mine or your own; if you can dance with wildness and let the ecstasy fill you to the tips of your fingers and toes without cautioning us to be careful, be realistic, or to remember the limitations of being a human.

It doesn't interest me if the story you're telling me is true. I want to know if you can disappoint another to be true to yourself; if you can bear the accusation of betrayal and not betray your own soul. I want to know if you can be faithless and therefore be trustworthy. I want to know if you can see beauty even when it is not pretty every day, and if you can source your life from ITS presence. I want to know if you can live with failure, yours and mine, and still stand on the edge of a lake and shout to the silver of the full moon, "YES!"

It doesn't interest me to know where you live or how much money you have. I want to know if you can get up after the night of grief and despair, weary and bruised to the bone, and do what needs to be done to feed the children.

It doesn't interest me who you are, how you came to be here. I want to know if you will stand in the center of the fire with me and not shrink back.

It doesn't interest me where or what or with whom you have studied. I want to know what sustains you from the inside when all else falls away. I want to know if you can be alone with yourself, and if you truly like the company you keep in the empty moments.

ORIAH MOUNTAIN DREAMER, "THE INVITATION"

We are usually confronted with going deeper inside ourselves when something momentous happens. In times of life transition—marriage, divorce, the birth of a child, the death of a parent or spouse, a major promotion or the loss of a job, a last child leaving home, a serious illness—our emotions and psychological responses are brought to the surface, and circumstances often compel soul searching.

At such times we can either face the music of our lives or shrink from the encounter and live a diminished existence.

Recently, I had an unparalleled opportunity to find out firsthand how it feels to be opened by life's betrayals and to discover what sustains me from the inside when all else falls away. Though I would not wish to repeat the experience, the lessons of the past year or so, like most unplanned excursions into the realm of personal psychology, taught me much about what really matters to me.

Before we travel together into this fertile but occasionally wild and woolly territory, let me share some of what I learned during my recent adventure in the psychological level of my interior mountain.

In June 1996, I returned home after receiving a distinguished award for scholarship and found my porch and lawn covered with reporters and camera crews looking for news of something that never happened. For almost a year and a half, I had served as a kind of intellectual sparring partner for First Lady Hillary Rodham Clinton, helping her focus ideas for the book she was writing.

A report that the First Lady and I had engaged in an imaginative exercise in which we reflected on what Eleanor

83

Roosevelt might have said about building a better society for our children sent the media scurrying for colorful copy. "Seance!" the front pages of the newspapers shouted. "Witchcraft!" And even that most dreaded of all epithets, "Guru!"

Needless to say, the distortions both embarrassed Mrs. Clinton and played havoc with my life and career. Virtually every newspaper and news magazine in the world carried the stories, the facts hugely distorted, and liberally dosed with snickering asides by reporters who never bothered to find out anything about me or my work.

As a result of this public ridicule, I found my reputation for thirty years of good work in the service of human betterment stained so badly that lectures were canceled by nervous sponsors and research grants were withdrawn. I felt that I had gone overnight from being regarded as a respected pioneer on the frontier of human capacities research to a laughable representative of the flaky fringe.

Yes, I received thousands of letters of support, and many people rose to defend me in letters to the editor and opinion columns. But this did little to relieve the pain I felt at so public a humiliation.

I was so hurt that I felt for a while that my career and usefulness were over and that I should simply remove myself from the public scene.

However, many people trusted me to continue with my work, to show strength and get on with it. This led me to think long and hard about what one does to recover the integrity of the self in the face of a devastating experience.

At the time of wounding it is difficult and yet absolutely essential to look at what happened in fresh ways.

First, we must stop repeating to ourselves and others the details of the events or people that caused us pain. We do this not to deny the facts but to push ourselves out of the seduction of tunnel vision into a broader landscape that can reveal potent opportunities for growth.

Then we ask ourselves hard questions: Are we in a cauldron of pain or a chalice of opportunity? Shall we fret and whine, or can we see our suffering as a hand coming from the Higher Power to pull us into a new story?

Finally, we tell our story again, not as a repetition of historical detail, but as a tale in which the wounding occurs in the middle, the ending of which is the birth of a new grace.

Personal wounding opens us, as nothing else can, to the larger reality that we contain. Suffering cracks the boundaries of what we thought we could stand. And yet, through these cracks sprout the seeds of healing and transformation.

Being more vulnerable ourselves, we reach out, extending our hands and our hearts to others who are suffering. As a result of my experience, I feel I can be more helpful to others who are seeking to revision their own traumas in profound and useful ways.

Aside from its personal psychological consequences, my brush with unexpected and unsolicited notoriety has led me to reflect on the larger meaning of what happened.

Why is it, I asked myself, that when a couple of intelligent women get together and use an inward-turning exercise to focus their thinking on a critical issue, the media goes

85

mad? After all, the exercise itself was rather ordinary, in line with psychological brainstorming techniques used regularly in think tanks and corporate boardrooms across the country. What was it that turned the evening news into an Inquisition?

I suspect that the answer lies in two great phobias—fear of the rising power of women and fear of the power of imagination and inner realities. Put them together and you have the Shadow of our age, a dread of methods and solutions based on human values rather than on materialistic ones.

As women rise to positions of influence, their mind style and way of working are coming more and more into the spotlight. Focusing on the journey more than simply on the destination, they solve problems by looking for ways to make things develop and grow from within rather than by imposing solutions from without. Most important, they are by and large comfortable with using the imagination to discover answers.

Since they don't understand these methods and thus cannot control them, the old minds of the existing power structure get frightened. In the case of Mrs. Clinton and myself, fear drove the media to make news out of what was really an attempt to solve hard problems in a new way and to right an ecological imbalance—our gross overuse of the outer world and underuse of the inner one.

It is wrong to trust only those answers that come from facts and statistics and to ridicule solutions that arise from imagination and intuition. It is wrong to regard ideas based in memory, reflection, and the creative nature of the psyche as dangerous fantasies and spooks.

The result of such outmoded thinking is what I sadly experienced—early Freud meeting old fundamentalism joined up with P. T. Barnum, on front pages and prime time.

We can no longer afford to live as if emotions, memories, and intuition were beside the point. The mainstream must tap into the deep stream of personal psychology in order to renew itself. To save ourselves and our world, each of us must work hard and humbly to acquire the inner capacities necessary for a deepened and empowered psychological and spiritual life.

How is this to be done?

For one thing, even when circumstances do not propel us into the psychological realm, we can initiate visits on our own. Familiarity with the territory—its glorious vistas as well as its mires and brambles—can help us bring awareness and energy to everyday events as well as to times of triumph or tragedy.

Let's begin our exploration of the psychological realm with laughter and a step back to view the human condition from a larger perspective.

I sometimes think advanced civilizations in the galaxy call our planet "the Skunkworks."

You know what the Skunkworks are, don't you?

The Skunkworks are a little laboratory far off the main drag where mad inventors try mad experiments. And if occasionally the experiment gets out of hand and stinks to high heaven, that's okay, because everybody expects the Skunkworks to smell, and a few of the crazy experiments even work.

Some precautions must be taken, however. This is why the planet Earth and its most dangerous species, human beings, have to be put way out at the end of a side arm of the Milky Way, far from the center of things. You can't run a decent galaxy with a Skunkworks right splat in the middle!

Now, what's the big experiment going on in our particular Skunkworks?

Kidding aside, I think that it's about creating Godseeds. In a rather miraculous way, the universe has conspired to give human beings enough resources to play with so that we can evolve ourselves into cocreators.

Cocreators are people like you and me who get in touch with their inner resources, figure out how to use them, and then take an active personal role in their Divine Father/Mother's business of world making.

World making can be a giant enterprise involving many people and institutions, or it can be very small and limited to one's immediate friends or family.

Or even to oneself.

The size of the eventual application makes little difference when it comes to the essential first step of gaining inner knowledge.

Psychological knowledge is not something you can buy. It doesn't come in a jar. It doesn't come through the internet. It doesn't even come in this book. Where it can come from is listening to and watching and learning from yourself in a special way.

There's no question that such listening and learning are hard work. But the potential payoff is enormous. For one thing, attention to the inner workings of our psyche can help us make creativity central to our lives.

They say that ideas are a dime a dozen. They are not.

Ideas are diamonds, and they are stocked and stored in the great structure that we call our mind-body system. Beneath the surface crust of ordinary consciousness, we are all filled with ideas and associations linking with other ideas—the very stuff of evolution moving in us to emerge as innovation.

Our deep mind is making associations all the time. It's just that we generally don't inhabit enough of ourselves to become aware of them.

What is it about people who do inhabit more of themselves? Why is it that they can take things from the outer world, put them together with things from the inner world, and create something new?

Part of the secret of creativity is learning to look at things in different ways. Children are very good at this, as their minds have not yet hardened into set patterns.

You may have heard of the little girl who had been trying for days to insert a rope-belt into her pajamas. One hot day she came in from playing and went to the freezer to get an ice cube. Looking at the ice cube, it occurred to her that if she wet the rope and froze it into a horseshoe shape, she could slide it through the open band of her pajamas.

When most of us tramp through the fields and get burrs on our pants, we pull them off, being careful not to let them stick to our fingers. But one man looked in a different way at those prickly burrs adhering to his trousers. Not too long after, he invented Velcro.

Johannes Gutenberg watched grapes being pressed and thought, What if you pressed letters that way? That was the beginning of the printing press, which led to this book and everything else you read.

Creativity has to do with really noticing the things that are without, letting them bloom in the great within, and being available to the possibility of novelty.

When I have studied creative people, I find that they think in many frames of mind. They don't just ponder a problem. They sift it through images as well as words. They feel it playing upon their bodies as well as their minds. They marinate themselves in the problem until it seems that the thing they are working on has almost acquired a personality of its own.

A problem percolates in the back of their minds while they go about their daily life. Things they see in the world that remind them of the problem are jotted down as grist for the creative mill. Then, one day, something emerges as a full-fledged possibility that demands to be tried, written, told, sung about, created.

Much the same process can be applied to anything you wish to accomplish.

Begin by giving yourself an intention—something you

want to do or discover. See this intention as an image—seen or felt, heard, touched, even tasted. Then dwell on images of future accomplishment, using as many of your interior senses as you can.

Soon you will find yourself sponsored by your image, activated by it, to the point that you will have the passion and the purpose to do something about it.

What's more, life itself will have a passion for you. You will be a cocreator.

Now, creativity doesn't have to lead to something. It doesn't have to result in a song, a dance, a novel, a better mousetrap. The greatest form of creativity is the re-creation of yourself. Moreover, the creative work you do on yourself will heighten your capacity for creativity in other things.

With this in mind, let's return to the interior mountain and journey to its second level, the psychological realm. Fasten your seat belts. This ride can be a roller-coaster.

91

Again, you find yourself on the path going up and around the mountain. Your senses are heightened as a result of your visit to the sensory level, and the pine scents on the mountain breeze tickle your nose pleasurably. The connections among senses are enhanced as well, and you seem to feel the birds' song on your skin when you hear it.

Since your last visit, mushrooms have sprouted on the path, and you bend to look at their reddish-brown caps and white gills. A strong earth smell fills your nostrils as you pick one for closer investigation.

You come once again to the stone tablet. This time you are more expert in lifting it off and easing yourself inside the mountain.

Walking down and around, you reach again the door to the sensory realm, this time smelling roses and baking bread. With a quick caress of the velvet panel, you move past and continue down and around until you come to the mirrored door, the entrance to the psychological realm. With a lingering glance at the many yous reflected in the mirror, you open the door and enter.

This time, someone is here to meet you. This person looks a lot like you, but like you would look if you had spent a thousand years developing your full potential. It is your Essential Self, your Guide—the part of yourself that is encoded with your higher destiny, your purpose for being, and manifests now as what you yet may be.

Some of you may see this being as representing the Soul itself—the deepest, holiest, most whole part of you.

Some may sense it as the inner strength and vital force that directs your life and growth toward becoming all you are capable of being.

Our Essential Self has a radiance that our local self does not. It is in touch with both our life and the Life of the Universe. It is in touch with the wisdom of the earth and the wisdom of the heart. It can put us in touch with the unexplored continents that lie within our minds and bodies, for it knows the maps of the soul and the treasures that can be found there.

The Essential Self knows the possible paths our life may

take and wants to help us choose the best ones. It knows how to turn imagination into reality and make the life we live fulfilling and creative. Above all, it knows why we are here and what we yet can do; where we can go and why we need to go there.

Closer than breathing, nearer than hands and feet, the Essential Self is the mysterious friend who has always been ever near, however much we have denied its existence.

From here on, let's just call this being "the Friend." Getting to know this Friend is a wonderful experience. One is never really "alone" again.

To help you to get a stronger sense of the Friend, I'd like you to try an imaginative exercise that may seem a little strange at first. But trust me; it works!

To begin, place an actual chair opposite you and "ask" the Friend to come and sit in that chair. Try to imagine what the Friend looks like, what he or she is wearing. Allow yourself to perceive a growing sense of the presence of the Friend sitting in the chair opposite you.

Still sensing the presence of the Friend, close your eyes for a moment and stretch your hands out, palms facing outward. Then imagine that the Friend, sitting opposite you, is also stretching out his or her hands.

See if you can sense, however subtly, the "hands" of the Friend touching yours. You may feel a slight breeze or a gentle electric sensation or perhaps an even more palpable impression.

As this sense of touching hands becomes more vivid, try to imagine with your inner eye and ear what the Friend may look like, sound like, be like. Again, let that sense of presence increase.

Open your eyes and try to maintain a sense of the presence of the Friend. Then close your eyes and do the same. Open them again, continuing to imagine the presence of the Friend.

Now let's do something that can help to make your sense of the Friend even stronger.

Stand up and move into the chair where the Friend was sitting. Now imagine that you are the Friend (which, actually, you are) looking and sensing the local version of "yourself" sitting opposite. Hold up your palms and sense the feel of the palms and the presence of "yourself."

As the Friend, sense what "you" look like, the feel of your hands, the play of light and shadow around "your" face. But sense "yourself" from the perspective of the understanding and compassionate Friend. Look upon the "person" sitting opposite you with the wisdom that comes from the soul's knowing, which is the Friend's knowing.

Now get up and sit in the opposite seat, returning to your own identity as you do so. Again, hold up your hands to the Friend, the sense of touch between your hands even stronger now. But this time, the sense of the presence of the Friend is growing more natural. You feel that, indeed, you are in the presence of a very wonderful Friend.

You might wish to go back and forth a few times, switching chairs, being yourself sensing the Friend and then being the Friend sensing and knowing you.

Is your sense of the Friend's presence more vivid now?

Now that you have a clearer perception of the Friend's being, travel with the Friend deeper into the psychological realm.

Just beyond the entrance, you may recall, is the pond of memory. Let's go there first.

A good memory is a valuable thing. It increases our intelligence and creativity by giving us access to the thousands of images and ideas that once were ours. It allows us to inhabit our lives more fully—to be present to the whole range of our experiences and not just dwell on the hot spots. Memory allows us to live the life we are given.

It is easy to learn to live within the treasure house of memory instead of watching memory continuously fade into the horizon like a retreating train. If you'd like to see what your memory treasure house contains, find a comfortable spot for you and your Friend to sit by the pond of memory, and let's begin.

Mist rises up from the pond of memory as seen or felt images, images that are memories from your life. The landscape here in the psychological realm encourages memory.

The presence of the Friend by your side also helps make the images clear. Whenever your memory seems dim or fleeting, ask the Friend to help make it stronger and more vivid, or become the Friend for a moment and see if that helps the memory become more real.

Imagine now that you are hearing a gentle voice that prompts you to remember scenes from your childhood. As the images rise from the pond, whether pictures or words or colors or tastes or smells, speak them out loud to the Friend if you like, or write them in a journal:

> Tell me about favorite foods from your childhood. . . .

> Tell me from your childhood about a game or a song that you remember. . . .

> Tell me from your childhood about a much-loved or much-hated teacher. . . .

> Tell me from your childhood about an animal you knew. . . .

> Tell me from your childhood about a very old man or woman. . . .

> Tell me from your childhood about a very young girl or boy you knew. . . .

> Tell me from your childhood about a vacation or a trip you took. . . .

Now the voice suggests that you remember scenes from other times of your life:

> Remember your high school graduation or its equivalent. . . .

> Remember getting up this morning. . . .

Remember the first time you fell in love or got a
crush on somebody. . . .

Remember a recent birthday party. . . .

Remember one of the best days you ever spent. . . .

Remember buying or getting this book. . . .

Remember the Friend sensing you. Remember you
sensing the Friend. . . .

As you activate childhood memories, chances are you are
also helping your memory banks become more generous
with their credit. You also regain something of the vividness
of childhood perceptions, because you are awakening the
memories of these perceptions, which add their luster to
your adult perceptions. By working with the memories of
other time zones in our lives, we retune all our senses.

You can practice your new memory skills in many interesting ways:

* Find a photograph of yourself as a child and look at it
  carefully. Close your eyes and remember everything
  you can about being the age you were in the picture.
  Then go out into nature and notice whether your perceptions have regained some of the freshness you
  knew as a child.

* Try the same exercise with a picture of your mother or
  father or even with the picture of a famous man or

woman you admire. See how much you "remember" about your father's life before you were born or about the life of a famous person you have never met.

Once your memory circuits are turned on, you can even "remember" real events that you did not witness. You may have read about these happenings or may have seen a movie or television show dealing with them, but remembering them imaginatively can make it seem as if you were really there.

Imaginative memory also enhances your creativity because it gives you practice in making associations in the theater of the mind. Strong links between memory and imagination help you to invent new material more easily.

Again, imagine that a voice prompts you to remember certain events. Speaking your recollections out loud will prime the pump of creative imagination. If you prefer, you may also write your responses in a journal.

98

Your Friend will help you to call up associations, because your Friend has direct access to all the things you have learned, seen, or imagined. You might also imagine that your Friend links you to the collective unconscious—the soul and memory of the whole human race.

Ready? Let's begin.

Remember sailing on the first voyage with Christopher Columbus. . . .

Now, please, remember the building of the Great Pyramid in ancient Egypt. . . .

Remember Joan of Arc leading the armies of France. . . .

Remember Francis of Assisi, talking to the birds. . . .

Remember Abraham Lincoln delivering the "Gettysburg Address.". . .

Remember Cleopatra sailing down the Nile in her perfumed golden barge. . . .

Remember dinosaurs eating the leaves off the tops of trees. . . .

Remember the creation of the Earth. . . .

Remember the creation of the universe. . . .

Now, don't worry about the logic, but remember yourself ten years from now. . . .

Remember this earth a million years into the future. . . .

Remember yourself totally at this present moment. . . .

It's easy to continue this practice yourself.

* Study an old photograph of people in the nineteenth century walking in the streets. Imagine yourself back in time, and put yourself in the scene.

* Make a visit to a museum an imaginative adventure in time travel. Dive into other eras, other lives, "remembering" yourself through the paintings as a grand lady of the French court, a saint, or even as the Holy Child. Imagine yourself into the famous painting of the signing of the "Declaration of Independence," and add your signature to the document. Stand behind the model as Leonardo da Vinci paints the *Mona Lisa*. Then go out to lunch with him.

* Reading a historical novel, discover yourself within the adventure, inventing different characters, different plots, even different endings than the one the author put on paper. Before long you may find that the novel-making skills of your mind demand expression, and stories and plots will teem within you.

Play with these practices often enough, and you will become an artist of "far memory."

Now, do you remember the creative intention you experienced with all your senses at the end of your journey to the sensory realm?

Again, imagine your intention coming to pass, but this time experience it even more vividly. Not only are all your senses engaged, but also you hold the vision of realizing your intention with a kind of imaginative clarity that makes it seem more real than before. By "remembering" your creative intention as it might develop in the near future, you put it more solidly into your life plan.

As you live out your intention again, note what new ideas and elements have been added. Note, too, how the intention may have changed and how it may seem more realistic in your mind, as if it already is happening. In a way, it *is* already happening, for in this exercise you are priming your passion for the possible, making the possible a more likely happening. So go to it, and imagine your intention as fully as you can. . . .

Congratulate yourself. You have patterned and prepared within for what you most desire to manifest in your life. What is more, the internal image of success you have generated makes you more likely to look for opportunities to work creatively toward fulfilling your intention. A vivid image helps give you the energy and focus to stick with it until your dream becomes reality.

101

Shall we move on now to another part of the psychological realm and see what it holds? Your wandering takes you past caverns of potential, rivers of thought, meadows thick with the flowers of emotions and moods.

Suddenly you hear a ticking, a chiming, the booming announcement of a large bell. Following the sounds, you come to the Temple of Time. The psychological realm is home to many kinds of time, as you will soon see.

Entering the temple, you discover a room filled to over-flowing with many kinds of timepieces. There's a sundial and an hourglass and an ancient water clock from China that lets drops of water fall at regular intervals. Look, there's a fourteenth-century church clock with an intricate system of ropes and pulleys.

Cuckoo clocks, Big Ben, pocket watches, stopwatches, wristwatches, alarm clocks, mantle clocks, grandfather clocks, and even an atomic clock that can keep track of tiny particles of time fill the room—timekeepers of every description.

Looking at all these clocks brings to mind the many kinds of time you know. What we think of as clock time is only a small part of your time experience.

Your body runs on biological time with its circadian rhythms that govern cycles of sleep and waking, digestion, respiration, and other natural functions.

You are also familiar with time flying when you're having fun, time crawling when you're bored, and even time standing still in moments of shock or wonderment. You regularly experience being out of time, wasting time, over-scheduled time, falling-in-love time, anxious time, meditation time, timeless time.

If you have ever been in a high creative moment or had a mystical or rapturous experience, you know what it is to feel eternity crack your usual categories of time.

Let us consider now what it would be like if we had all the time in the world to play with. Actually we do, and learning to use time in many different ways is one of our greatest untapped potentials.

To begin our play with time, let's try an exercise in which our newly honed skill at inner imagery can help us experience as much in a few minutes as might normally take an hour, a day, or even longer.

As you have discovered, images are not only visual. They can also be kinesthetic—felt in the body as muscular sensations. They can be auditory or hearing images or even images to be tasted or smelled. Images can also be combinations of sensations, and they can be grasped and known in an imaginative or intuitive way.

When we think in images, our brain seems to need less time to reach a conclusion, relive an event, or rehearse a skill than it does when we think in the ordinary way. Some scientists believe that this time shortcut happens because thinking in images involves greater use of the right hemisphere of the brain, which does not process time in a linear, one-thing-after-another fashion.

Let me show you what I mean. Choose something from the following list that you wish to explore in images:

* Take a wonderful trip to a new place, or revisit a place you have traveled to in the past.

* Investigate a project related to your work.

* Plan and cook a complicated and delicious meal.

* Redecorate your room or your whole house.

Have you decided on something?

Now, let's say that you have one minute of clock time to perform this exercise. In that minute you will close your eyes and experience as many scenes or events or thought pictures related to the trip or project or meal or house as you can. You may wish to set an egg timer or have a friend hold a watch.

Close your eyes and allow the one minute to begin now. . . .

Time's up! Subjectively speaking, how much time seems to have gone by?

Some of you may feel that it was hours or months or even years. Others might say that the interval seemed timeless. Even if you experienced the time as only a minute or less, how many different images did you see?

In the world of subjective time, internal time can be experienced to fill up the record of many hours. You can encounter faces and places all over the globe—the Great Wall of China, a beach in the Antilles, playing street football outside your old high school, a wedding, the birth of a child—any event you ever or never experienced.

Once you gain access to the varieties of time, you can rehearse and improve skills with rapidity and have all the time you need for what you wish to do. Most important, you will discover time to be a friend and not an enemy.

Actually, we stretch time as well as shorten it all the time, but rarely are we aware of it. A neat trick for working with time consciously is to imagine a yardstick, thirty-six inches long. Think of the first twelve inches as time past, the middle twelve inches as time present, and the last twelve inches as time future.

Now, in your imagination, shorten the past and the present to eight inches each, and stretch the future to twenty inches. Actually visualize the segments of the ruler expanding or contracting. What changes do you notice in your body and your perceptions when the future is stretched? Perhaps you feel a sense of ease, as if you have all the time you need to do whatever you want. What a wonderful way to reduce stress on a busy day!

Now, let's stretch the past. Again picture the yardstick of time. In your mind's eye, shrink the future to eight inches, keep the present at eight inches, and extend the past to twenty inches. Do you see yourself now as standing on the peak of a huge mountain of experiences? Are you more aware of your roots and of the weave of interconnections between people and things?

For our final experiment, let's shrink the past and the future to three inches and stretch the present to thirty inches. Now look around. Are your surroundings energized and loaded with presence? Note, too, whether your energy level has increased. A radically extended present is a good state to cultivate when you need to concentrate on something.

The next time you are sitting through a boring lecture or meeting, call the yardstick of time to mind and use it to stretch your sense of time past. Often you will find that the lecture seems shorter. When you are having a great time with a special friend, on the other hand, stretch out the future on the yardstick to give yourself the perception of endless hours of enjoyment.

With practice you can become quite proficient and learn to speed up or slow down time at will!

Having more subjective time also gives you more time to rehearse and remember joy. Remembering joy opens you to better relationships, deeper understanding, and more appreciation of life. And you stop boring God.

Let's try another of these time games now. Take another minute of clock time in which to remember an incident from your life that gave you considerable joy. Use all your senses and imaginative faculties and live in that place of remembered joy as if you were still there. Stay in that state of joy for the entire minute. . . .

Returning now, how do you feel?

Rehearsing joy is a way to build a life of appreciation. I find that when I am really down, the practice of remembering joy gives me a truer perspective on my life.

Too often we fall into the pattern of remembering only sorrows or painful moments. Focusing on negativity increases our sensitivity to pain and fixates us more intensely on whatever difficulty comes our way. Keep this pattern up, and we move from chronic hurt to cynicism to paranoia and to thinking that the world has it in for us.

Rehearsing joy has quite the opposite effect. Try applying what the Buddhists call mindfulness to your thoughts. When an unhappy memory or toxic thought starts to cross your mind, say, "Stop!" and reframe that thought to remembering joy.

If you can't quite do that, then try practicing gratitude for everything that you have and everything that you are. Gradually, you will rebuild your mind into a city of light instead of one of dark alleys and cul-de-sacs.

The practice of gratitude for whatever the day brings reveals the side of life beyond the shadows. As I look

106

around, I am grateful for the beauty of the plant by the table, the sound of my husband's voice downstairs, the intelligence of my black-and-white kitten, Boxer, who is sitting here, as I write, figuring out how to untie knots in my shoelaces.

Look around you now and notice what you are grateful for. You may see large things or small ones—a pattern of light on the wall, a person or pet, a concept, a state of being, a world—whatever. If you like, name a number of such things out loud and explain why you are grateful that they are in your life. You might also jot down a list in your journal.

Note the change in your mind and body as you practice gratitude. If you really want to change your life, commit yourself to practicing gratitude each day. You will sense the dimensions of things more clearly, empower people more readily, and find yourself a more enthusiastic participant in this remarkable world.

Your memory and creativity may also improve because you attend to things more closely when you are in a state of gratitude.

Why?

Because you appreciate them.

Several times a year or more you might give an "Appreciation Party" for friends or people you admire and want to celebrate.

You may want to add to the general well-being by writing a letter whenever you feel the urge to thank someone for an accomplishment. Whenever I enjoy a piece of writing, I write to the author and thank them for their work. I try to do the same for people who have put their lives on the line, like nurses, social workers, teachers, and, yes, even a few politicians.

Having spent time in "high places," I have been shocked to discover how little appreciation people in public life actually get. They read empowering letters with a joy and gratitude that is astonishing.

Speaking of people for whom you might be thankful, your Friend has an idea. Now might be a good time to meet again some of your inner crew and learn how they can help you in your daily life. You walk quickly along the path through the forest until you come to the clearing where your particular crew is awaiting you.

Look around and see or sense their loving presence. It's a wonderful thing to have so many willing inner helpers, so many masters of varied skills and attitudes—Cook, Painter, Plumber, Psychologist, Healer, Mechanic, Accountant, Inventor, Poet, Relationship Expert, Parent, Orator, Lover, Student, Teacher, Theologian, Traveler, Meditator, Comedian, Animal Companion, House Cleaner, Writer, Singer, Group Organizer, Group Member, Time Manager, Mystic, Compassionate One.

There are many others who only you would know. Some hold the mastery of a particular skill that you have, like swimming or playing the violin or weaving or woodworking.

Others represent your various roles and relationships— daughter, sister, best friend, best buddy, mentor.

108

Anything with which you have familiarity and practice, however small or large, has an inner expert who is always available to support, consult, and inspire your outer efforts.

Would you like to try a sample consultation?

Choose a skill you would like to work on, and ask the master of that skill to come forward. This being leads you to a place nearby where you can work together to improve your skill. All the materials you need are there—paints, piano, golf clubs, tennis rackets, computers, dancing shoes—whatever you need.

The very space around you seems filled with the essence of your skill. At this level of the psyche, an enormous amount of information is available that is not normally processed by the conscious mind. Your inner master of a skill has access to all the knowledge that you ever gleaned, consciously or unconsciously, about the skill, as well as some new tricks. When you call on the master, some of this hidden knowledge can be harvested and integrated into your learning.

Let's see how this works.

The master of the skill may communicate with you with words or without them. Perhaps the teaching will feel like a muscular sensation or will appear as a sudden intuitive knowing. You may be advised to practice old skills, or you may be taught new ones. However it happens, this being who holds the mastery will give you deep and potent instructions. As you receive this intensive training, you will feel increasingly free, spontaneous, and confident, even overcoming any inhibitions or blocks that you had.

You will be working with subjective time in this exercise, so get an egg timer or have a friend hold the time for you.

Give yourself five minutes of clock time, which is equal subjectively to all the time you need. In these minutes or hours or days, you will have a rich learning session with the master of the skill, rehearsing and improving your skill. Close your eyes and begin. . . .

Coming back now, notice how you feel in your body. Is the skill more a part of you? Do you have a greater feeling of pleasure and confidence about it? Are you looking forward to performing it?

In fact, if it is possible for you actually to engage in the skill now, please do so and notice if technical improvements have taken place. Practicing with the inner master is something you can do over and over again.

After a while, you will not have go through the steps to call up this member of your crew. The inner expert will be so much a part of you, it will be as if you are receiving instructions and improvements whenever you practice.

You can employ the same procedure to call upon other members of your inner crew who have mastery in other skills or qualities of excellence. If you give time and practice to rehearsing skills on the inner level, their outer manifestations will grow in you more quickly.

Even skills relevant to communication and improved relationships can be gained using this process.

You might wish to try this by calling upon the Relationship Expert now. This member of your inner crew offers you the gift of communion, of getting in touch with the Essential Self of someone you know instead of continually getting bogged down in tired old patterns of relating.

Here's a way such a session might work. Bring to mind a person with whom you would like to get along better. Use all of your senses to make the image of this person clear in your imagination—his or her appearance, voice, habits, attitudes, ways of being.

Imagine now that the Relationship Expert takes you and this person to a special couch where you can relax and talk together.

Now, perhaps, the Expert suggests that you and the person you have brought to mind engage in conversation about the issues that divide you. In reality, of course, you will be taking both parts in this imaginary conversation. Letting go of your preconceptions about the other person and actually speaking in his or her voice can give you many insights.

If you reach a stalemate in your conversation, ask the Relationship Expert to help you move beyond the stuck place. For instance, the Expert might point out that you and your friend or relation are really each other's teacher, honing and refining each other by your very differences.

Under the Relationship Expert's guidance, you might then imagine that you are holding the hand of the other person and seeing deeply into his or her essential nature. At the same time, the person you are seeking to get along with better is seeing deeply into your mind and heart. If emotions arise, allow them to deepen the communion. Cry if you need to, and allow yourself to be comforted by your friend or relation.

111

When you feel your session is complete for now, ask the Expert to continue to help in your relationship. Promise yourself that whenever you can, you will try to bring this attitude of deep listening and communion into an actual meeting with your friend.

The Friend now takes you by the hand and leads you back to meet with the rest of your inner crew. Among them, you may feel particularly drawn to working with the Healer.

You might think of the Healer as the representative of your innate body wisdom and intuition, the part of yourself that has access to billions of bits of information about your health and its improvement.

By allowing the essence of the Healer to occupy the forefront of your consciousness, you can gain a better sense of what you need to do for yourself to achieve and maintain your best state of health.

If you wish to consult your inner Healer, take his or her hand and gaze deeply into the Healer's eyes. Ask the Healer what you can do to improve your health. The answers may come in words or images, feeling states or strong hunches.

Depending on what you need at the moment, you might ask practical questions about symptoms—whether to have them treated or let them be. You can ask for advice on diet and exercise. Most important, you can ask for a strong impression of how it would feel to be in your optimally functioning body.

Working with your Healer in this way is actually something we do all the time. If you're a parent, don't you often "know" when your child's stomachache needs medical attention or just a hug? A consultation with your inner Healer allows you to apply the same type of intuition to yourself.

You can get in touch with other aspects of your natural inner knowing by working with other members of your inner crew—the Inventor, the Lover, the Student, the Writer, the Group Organizer, the Mystic. As you face each one, you may have a sense of strongly identifying or even merging for a few moments, gaining something of the particular ability that this part of yourself holds.

If the idea of having so many "beings" within yourself seems strange, it's because our culture puts so much emphasis on each person having a single, consistent personality or role. We tend to see ourselves through a single lens as a lawyer, a teacher, or a homemaker, as if that single label expresses all of what we are. We describe our personality as "outgoing" or "quiet and shy," as "friendly" or "solitary," as if these terms express all of what we are or can be. Our other interests, the other parts of ourselves, we trivialize by calling them "hobbies," or we seldom consider them as aspects of ourselves at all.

On the inner level, this emphasis on a unified personality translates into a limited "local ego" against which we measure and weigh every new experience and challenge. "Does this new activity or person strengthen my local ego, my sense of who I am?" we ask ourselves. If so, we embrace it and add it to our self-conception. If it threatens the unified fortress of the self, we brand the new experience or person as an outcast and drive it away.

How many opportunities for growth and enrichment do we deny ourselves by thinking of ourselves in this limited way? What new skills, new friends or associates, new experiences do we miss because they seem on the surface to be "out of character" for us?

There is, however, another way to be. What we think of as "personality" changes from one era or culture to another. Among many indigenous peoples, our emphasis on satisfying the desires and wishes of a unified local ego is regarded as just plain crazy!

In Bali, for example, people move with ease to inhabiting different parts of themselves. In the course of a week, a Balinese man might be a rice farmer, a mask maker, a musician in the orchestra, a dancer or player in the ritual dramas, a textile designer, and a member of some service club, while still being very much devoted to all generations of his family. Each of these roles is "who he is," and each is given full emphasis and attention while it is being performed.

The Balinese ideal of a fluid and multiple personality might be a model for the healthier psyche we all can aspire to as we develop greater access to the populations of our own inner space.

If schizophrenia, the splitting or fragmentation of the personality, is the disease of the modern human condition, then "polyphrenia," gaining access to the varied parts of our personality, can represent our extended health. Indeed, in a world of growing encounters with many different cultures and ways of being, the way to avoid being overwhelmed is to have an active congregation of personalities within us to draw upon.

If you wish to explore the richness of an extended self, become polyphrenic in practice as well as in personality.

Try taking a class in something you never thought you might do—like auto mechanics or belly dancing or wild mushroom hunting. I've recently taken up baseball pitching. A much-esteemed American Hindu spiritual leader of my acquaintance is learning to play hockey.

New and unusual skill building has a wonderful way of expanding the range and attributes of your various selves.

Also included in our internal congregation are beings that seem to be ourselves at earlier ages. Popularized (and ridiculed) by such names as "the inner child," these earlier versions of our self have been reached through a variety of procedures, including hypnosis, meditation, inward focusing, and even electrical stimulation of the brain.

Why would we want to get in touch with such beings? What good can they do us today?

The trick is that these earlier versions of ourselves are often caught in attitudes and woundings we experienced at earlier times in our life. There they are, our younger selves, trapped in a kind of time warp, playing out the same sad stories over and over again. They do not know that we have grown up and moved on, and they persist in projecting old traumas into our current mindstream.

Visiting an earlier version of yourself as friend and wise counselor, you may be able to provide comfort or to heal some of their pain and, in so doing, to redirect the patterns and emotional coloring of your present mind.

You might wish to take your Friend along to the meeting, since he or she holds the totality of your life and memories, or to include some other members of your inner crew in the greeting party, perhaps the Psychologist, the Parent, or the Healer.

Take a moment to think of some times in your life when it would have been very healing for you to have been visited by your present self, who is possessed of the wisdom and understanding you've acquired in the intervening years.

For the sake of this initial exercise, it may be better not to choose times when you were caught up in trauma. Rather, look for periods of confusion or conflict, when a wise and compassionate adviser would have been much appreciated.

Ready? Let's begin.

I have found it effective actually to walk backward as you travel back in time to meet yourself at earlier stages. Playing soft meditative music also supports the process of this journey.

We begin close to the present. Think of a time in the last decade or so when you needed a friend to offer encouragement and psychological nourishment. Traveling back in your mind, call upon this person who was you to reveal himself or herself.

Bring the picture of this earlier self to mind as vividly as possible. See him or her as standing in front of you. Take this being by the hands and, supported by whatever members of your wise crew you have brought along, talk with your earlier self, giving the encouragement and empowerment that he or she might need.

If the self of this stage needs to release pain through tears or an angry outburst, hang in there in friendship and high witness. As your younger self begins to feel more secure, help him or her to see the positive consequences that have resulted from being hurt or stuck, and offer the perspective of your current experience and wisdom. . . .

When this part of the process seems complete, ask this earlier self to join you as you visit yourself at a still earlier age, perhaps some time in your twenties.

Again, walking backward, come upon yourself at a time in your early adulthood when you really needed a wise counselor. Perhaps this self is confused about the choice of a profession or a partner. Be there as a wise counselor. Tell your earlier self about how things have turned out, about the joys and satisfactions that have come into your life because of the difficult decision he or she made. . . .

When this part of the process seems finished, begin walking backward again, taking your young adult along to call upon yourself as an adolescent.

Listen to the adolescent that was you, full of hopes and dreams and fears, embarrassments and yearnings. Feel the wounds that your growing soul may have suffered. Assure the adolescent that the wounds of today are the strength of tomorrow. Give this young person the courage to be. Tell

117

him or her that life moves on and that more tools for living will be available in the future. . . .

Taking your adolescent along, travel still further back, to a time when you, as a very young person, could have used an older and wiser friend. Surprisingly, this child that is you takes your presence for granted.

"Of course," he or she might say, "you're myself grown up. Who are the rest of these guys?"

Introduce all of your other selves and sit down with the child to talk about what's going on in his or her life. If your child feels lonely or unappreciated, give support and empowerment; talk about the child's own talents and strengths. Give the child a sense of wonder about his or her body and mind and the treasures they contain. . . .

As a final step backward, invite the child to join you and the rest of your crew to visit yourself as a baby.

Experience now the wonder of cradling your infant self in your arms. Gazing upon the infant that was you with joy and tenderness, give your holy child the blessing of all your lives. Let the infant bask in the security and love that you bring, gifts that are the equivalents of gold, frankincense, and myrrh. . . .

Your Friend now turns, looks at you intently, and says, "Would you like to take a moment to contribute to the design of your life?"

"Of course!" you reply.

"Then follow me."

The Friend steps across what seems like an abyss. At first, you are nervous because there appears to be nothing but emptiness beneath you. But then the ground firms up under your feet, and you are led into a chamber that exists outside of time and space, where the great Pattern Keepers lay down the possibilities for each life.

Perhaps you envision your Pattern Keepers as weavers, entwining the many cords and colors of emotion and experience. Think carefully now about what fabric or thread of possibility you most want to weave into the tapestry of your life.

Is it a thread of opportunity? The silk of relationship? The nubby wool of challenge? Or perhaps it is the satin of comfort and reasonable abundance?

You may wish to consult with your earlier selves to help you choose a wise and fruitful pattern. Then, when you think you've got it, describe the new design to the Pattern Keepers. Watch and feel it being placed into your life, for this is the place of new genesis.

Bidding the Pattern Keepers farewell, begin to walk forward in time now, blessing yourself at each age with this new pattern of empowerment.

As you reach your current age, you see a figure approaching from the distance. It is a very wise old person. As he or she comes closer, you see that it your future self. This wise old person embraces you and gives you strength, grace, and courage from the future.

The wise old one speaks to you of the wonderful roads ahead and gives you some advice on taking them. Listen carefully and learn. . . .

What can we say about this process?

Of course, nothing that you have done changes the things that really happened in your life. However, you have done something equally wonderful. You have enriched the track of your experience.

We know that the episodes of our life are coded in the brain. But the brain does not make much distinction between what historically happened and how a memory has been reshaped or reimagined. As a result of this exercise, your memories of what happened have been joined to new memories of comfort and healing, encouragement and empowerment.

After working through this process, many of my students report feeling that they have gained a larger mind and a greater sense of soul. Old fears and deficiencies fade away. In giving themselves a "deepened past," they have reloomed their memories, adding rich layers of friendship and wise counsel that they can draw on in the future.

You may need to repeat the exercise a number of times in order to get its full value. You are doing real brain work here—modifying the track of the past as it is imprinted in your cells, releasing bad habits, freeing new mind, bringing energy and soul back to times when they may have been lost.

The glory of our minds is that we can time-travel in ourselves, entering into a point of pain to begin the process of releasing and healing it. Each time we face our woundings with recognition and acceptance, we heal them a bit more,

120

empowering and encouraging ourselves not to fall again and again into the black hole of despair.

But now it is time to leave the psychological realm, out through the mirrored door and up and around the interior mountain. Passing the door to the sensory realm and taking a swipe of chocolate mousse, you continue up until you reach the top, pull yourself out, and replace the stone tablet.

As you travel down and around the outside of the mountain, you marvel at the wonders of the mind and its abilities, and you vow to make many forays into its interior. But for now, you return to where you began, from which, shortly, another exploration will begin.

Did you know you were the
Mything Link?

Well, you are.

You are the living connection
between the great stories of all
times and places and the playing
out of these stories in everyday life.
Beneath the soil of your everyday
world lies the vast root system of the
Once Was and the Could Be.

You will feel this if you have
ever gone in quest of something—
a new job, a place where you feel
at home, a lost love, a new way of
being.

In every quest, you have wan-
dered with Percival in search of the
Grail, followed the yellow brick
road with Dorothy trying to get
back to Kansas, labored with Psyche
to be reunited with Eros, discovered

with Luke Skywalker the secrets of using the Force, meditated with Buddha under the bodhi tree, determined to reach enlightenment.

Storytelling is the oldest form of teaching and the basic vehicle for the transmission of culture from one generation to the next.

Cast yourself back five thousand years or more to your own ancestors, gathered around a flickering fire, huddled against the cold. Your great-grandmother many times back begins a story of being lost in a dark forest. Your great-uncle many times back picks it up and tells of strange beasts seen, walking spirits encountered, magic talismans discovered. Your great-niece, many times back, shudders in fear and delight, draws closer, and asks, "What happened next?"

This scene has been repeated many times down through the generations of your family, until today you gather around the flickering screen of the TV or movie theater, thrilling to a tale of long, long ago in a galaxy far, far away, where in the dark reaches of outer space heroes encounter allies glorious in their wisdom and with them battle the forces of darkness.

Story is the juice through which consciousness and culture move.

If Jesus had taught in long, dry lectures instead of in parables, do you think anyone would have listened?

If the great epics of the Mahabharata and the Ramayana were not marinated in the soul of India, would the culture be as fertile in spiritual riches?

If a visitor from another planet came down and asked the human race, "What exactly are you?" we would have to reply, "We are storytellers."

Stories are the currency of human growth. As they are told and retold, heard and reheard, they reveal their deeper meaning.

All of us intuitively know the power of story. We swap stories with our friends and family, often the same story again and again.

An old friend says, "Have I ever told you about . . . ?"

You reply, "Of course, but tell me again," for in each telling, the facts become more clear, the gold of meaning is refined, and new light is reflected into shadowed corners.

Moreover, how we view our life as a story often determines how life treats us.

If we see our life as a trivial story, we fall easily into inertia and defeat. Seeing our life as a larger story puts us back on our feet and helps us get on with living.

And seeing our life as a great story can fill us with the passion for the possible, give us access codes to a new-range of possibilities, and grant us a mythic life.

Here's an example of what I mean. A woman I know saw the story of her life as a play with an unhappy ending. Her children had grown and left home, her husband was caught up in his business, and her life consisted of seeing the same people and doing the same things. Without an engaging story, without a sense of her life going anywhere, she felt herself to be slowly dying of inertia.

Then one day a friend sent her a greeting card. Inside was a poem by Emily Dickinson:

I would not paint—a picture—
I'd rather be the One
It's bright impossibility
To dwell—delicious—on—
And wonder how the fingers feel
Whose rare—celestial—stir
Evokes so sweet a Torment—
Such sumptuous—Despair—

Nor would I be a Poet—
It's finer—own the Ear—
Enamored—impotent—content
The License to revere,
A privilege so awful
What would the Dower be,
Had I the Art to stun myself
With Bolts of Melody.

125

When she saw the words "sumptuous despair," she thought to herself, "How wonderful to rise out of my piddling desperation to a sumptuous celebration of my condition!"

She began to think of richer words to describe her feelings: "the arctic winter of my soul," "fields lying fallow with failed life," "desert dry kisses in the oasis of the heart."

Then she remembered that as a teenager she used to write poetry. She began to write again, about everyday things.

"I'm not sure my poems are exactly 'bolts of melody,'" she told me, "but thinking of myself as a poet kept me going."

"What happened next?" I asked.

"I sent a poem to my married daughter, and she responded with a poem of her own. Soon we were talking regularly on the phone and getting closer than we had been in years.

"Then one day, in a dead space in the conversation, I offered to read one of my poems to my friends. They were intrigued, and within a week we had a poetry-writing circle. We started to express and explore feelings as we never had before.

"One thing led to another, and soon I was creating poetry circles for church groups in my area. My life had grown larger."

Within a year, this woman was invited to create poetry-writing circles for inner-city women. She volunteered to be a Friend in Court for teenage girls in trouble and became a social activist trying to help families.

Her life today is somewhat harrowing, full of adventures, and she wouldn't give it up for anything.

"Now I do stun myself with bolts of melody," she says. "And I bring melodies into places where people had forgotten that there was a song to life."

By moving from a small to a larger to a great story for her life, this woman turned a key and opened the locked doors of her soul. She now lives a life that can only be called mythic.

This story demonstrates how easily one can be drawn into myth. Its potent language, its symbols and images are all around us, charged with significance and purpose. Myth tells of the struggle to breathe new life into a dead land, the death of the soul and its resurrection, the search for the beloved, the great wound that turns one into a great healer.

Myths are great stories that have been told so often over so many years by so many people with so many cultural variations that they have become part of the structure of human consciousness.

Or perhaps it would be more accurate to put it the other way around.

Myths express so well the deep coding of human consciousness that people of all times and all places have felt compelled to tell and retell them to express the deepest truths they know about themselves.

Consciously or unconsciously, we are drawn to stories that provide the missing parts to the puzzle of our own life. When we encounter these tales, we recognize them instantly. There is something about them, a flash of connection that says, "In this story is a piece of my own."

Joseph Campbell, who probably understood myth better than any other figure in our century, put it best: "The symbols of mythology are not manufactured; they cannot be ordered, invented, or permanently suppressed. They are spontaneous productions of the psyche, and each bears within it, unchanged, the germ power of its source."

Nobody escapes myth, hard as one may try, ordinary as one's life may seem. Humans, in heart and soul, are mythic beings. Coded in our very cells, story breeds in our bones, cools in our blood, travels in our nervous system, incarnates with us in the womb, weaves through the roles and rituals of our lives, celebrates in our triumphs, grieves in our tragedies.

From its very inception, our life is a great story, a true myth. Each of us is grown in part from the sperm that made it—the heroic one of millions who battled its way upstream against insuperable odds to come together with its cosmic other half, only to die gloriously in an explosion of new life.

Every adolescent yearns for the land over the rainbow, the magical country of adulthood where we will shed our gawkiness, take on important tasks, be seen for who we really are, and find the glorious other who is our soul's companion.

The typical midlife crisis is a kind of passion play. We lose a job, our marriage falls apart, we face serious illness. This stripping away of our hopes and dreams often seems a kind of death.

But as happens in myths, our suffering occurs in the middle of the story, the end of which is access to greater skills and understanding and even resurrection into a new way of being.

Death, too, is a mythic transformation—not an end but the crossing of another threshold, an adventure into the Great Mystery, where we join our energy to the Originating Place from which all great stories come.

Myth is the immense gift the universe has given us to help us on our way through the obstacle course of life.

128

When we are reminded of and reconnected to the stories of generations past, a rich and varied world of experience opens to us.

Great stories allow our lives to be writ larger. When we reframe our life story as a great story or enter consciously into myth's potent dramas, we find new metaphors for conflict and conciliation, we strengthen our personal shields, we discover power objects to protect us from hurt, and we forge new bonds with glorious inner allies.

Myth is like a force field charging the incidents of our personal history with meaning and significance. It sustains and shapes our emotional attitudes, provides us with life purposes, and energizes our everyday acts. It gives life meaning and momentum.

When we link our lives with the experiences of mythic characters, we inherit a cache of experience that illumines and fortifies our own. We soon discover that we, too, are valuable characters in the drama of the world soul, pushing the boundaries of our own local story and gaining the courage to be and do so much more.

We are regrown to greatness, and we take our place with Percival and Penelope, with White Buffalo Woman and the Lady of the Lake, with Quetzalcoatl and Bridget and Mr. Spock.

The name of new character we forge out of great story is You. And the name of the myth is Your Story.

Now if you are ready to explore the ways story can enter and energize your life, then travel in your mind to the mountain of the self to descend to the level of myth.

So here you are again, walking up the mountain. There is more to you than there was at the beginning of this journey—more sense and sensibility, a larger physical and emotional capacity, more parts to your personality. You enjoy the smell of the pine woods, the crunch of pebbles, leaves, and earth beneath your feet, the dappling light of the sun through the high trees, the bracing wind as you climb higher.

You reach the top and remove the stone tablet. You are still not quite able to read its inscription, but something in you tells you that you are getting closer to deciphering its message.

You are filled with a strange excitement. This trip down the interior passageway seems even more of a journey, a visit to a place very familiar and yet filled with the promise of new discoveries.

You pass the delectable door to the Realm of the Senses, feeling your senses heightened as you do so. You pass the mirrored entrance to the Realm of the Psyche, pausing to take a look.

This time you are not alone in the reflection. Many members of your inner crew seem to be standing by your side. One comes forward, steps out of the mirror, and joins you. It is the Essential Self, the one we are calling the Friend. The Friend is in a humorous mood and seems to know something that we don't. Holding the Friend's hand is another member of your crew, a lively child who insists on coming along.

Led by the Friend, you and the child continue down and around the spiral pathway until you come to the richly carved door to the Realm of Myth and Symbol.

Chiseled there are the labors of Hercules, the tales of Arthur and Guinevere, the Hindu epic of Rama and Sita, the Navajo story of Spider Woman and her creation of the five worlds. The Grail looms larger than before and seems to emit a light that projects the faces of heroes and heroines from time out of mind.

You open the door and are enveloped in a buzz of frantic activity. A burly, bearded, red-headed man in ancient costume is shifting oars and unfurling the sails of a wooden seagoing vessel. A knight is cinching the saddle on his prancing stallion, preparing for a journey. A young girl with a little dog at her heels is looking up with yearning at the sky. A young Hindu man and woman are weeping as they leave a golden city.

Bewildered, you turn to the Friend. "Who are these people? What's going on here?"

"They are some of the great mythic heroes and heroines at the beginning of their stories," the Friend replies. "That burly man is Odysseus getting ready to sail from Troy. The knight is Percival setting out on the quest for the Grail. The little girl is Dorothy dreaming of the land over the rainbow. That handsome couple are Rama and Sita. They are being banished from their kingdom and will spend fourteen years living in the forest.

"If you look further, you will see many more, for we are in the realm of mythic beginnings."

"What do we do here?" you ask the Friend.

"You join the journey," the Friend replies, "and discover how these stories are really your story writ large—the lessons learned your lessons, the trials and adventures your own in fancy dress.

"Choose one to begin the journey today, knowing that you can always come back another day and make a different choice."

"How can I choose? They all look so inviting."

Suddenly the child holding your hand pulls you toward a scene you hadn't noticed before. A young man with a shock of blond hair is kicking a temperamental machine in a desert landscape.

"I know that story," the child breaks in. "That's Luke Skywalker. Let's see what happens to him."

"What fun!" you say and follow along.

"A good choice," the Friend says. "The child in you knows that something important is happening in this story that has relevance to your life and even to the culture at large. The *Star Wars* story is the hero's journey in its most recent and popular incarnation, a classic tale tricked out in high-tech gear.

"The journey of Luke Skywalker and his allies is the return of the hero with a thousand faces. It can help you discover the many faces you contain and the many stories as well."

"What do you mean by the hero's journey, and who is the hero with a thousand faces?" you ask.

The Friend explains. "Do you remember when you first visited the Realm of Myth and Symbol? You made a quick trip through the stages of the hero's journey: the Call to Adventure, the Gathering of Allies, Crossing the Threshold into the Realm of Amplified Power, the Belly of the Whale, the Road of Trials and Adventures, Meeting the Higher Parent and the Beloved Partner, Gaining a Great Boon, and then Returning as Master of Two Worlds.

"This pattern is found through most of the world's great myths, for it is embedded in the human psyche as well as in the stages of our evolution. Thousands of heroes and heroines of great story go through these stages. If your life story is to be heroic, you must pass through them as well. Let's enter this universal story now and see where it takes us."

Suddenly you feel very warm. You look up and see two suns burning in a pale blue sky. You are no longer on Earth but on the dusty planet of Tatooine. Your body is that of a wiry twenty-year-old boy. Your mood is complete frustration. Here you are, stuck on a podunk planet, doing a job you detest, with not much hope of escape.

You desperately yearn for something—anything—to happen. All your friends have left. If only your uncle would let you leave the farm and go off, as your father did, to become a pilot. Still your uncle insists that you stay "just one more season," as he insisted last year and the year before that and will undoubtedly insist next year and the year after that.

You feel life burgeoning within you. Unused and unknown skills are waiting to emerge. But how can that happen?

How many stories begin in a wasteland, where hopes are thwarted, rigid forms are imposed, and young people are discounted? In *The Wizard of Oz,* the movie version of the myth of sixty years ago, another frustrated young person is caught in the middle of a dustbowl. The gray sameness of the Kansas landscape symbolizes her frustration, dust and soil without soul.

Like Luke's aunt and uncle, Dorothy's are careworn and chronically worried. Like Luke, Dorothy yearns for a deeper, truer place, where the dreams that she dares to dream really do come true. But it will take a disaster from the skies to move Dorothy and Luke out of their stuck place and onto the high road of adventure.

Chances are, this is a familiar scene, and not just from the movies. It finds its way into your own life, when you are caught in a gray world of sameness with the sad sense of no way out.

Great story reminds us that life provides these "no exit" situations to build up our charge for finding a way off the planet of despair, over the rainbow to new possibilities.

Close your eyes for a minute and remember a time when you were stuck like Luke and Dorothy. What was going on? Call up the memory. Walk around in it. Write about in your journal for a few minutes, if you wish. Feel its feelings again, and remember how it was to be so stuck and so frustrated.

All wasteland situations, yours as well as Luke's and Dorothy's, contain in embryo the loaded time, a magical opportunity to seize the day and turn it around. But it generally takes a radical shift in consciousness to do this, for it's not always evident which path to take. Often one has to be moved out of stuckness by circumstances and outrageous forces.

Let's see how this happened to Luke and remember how it may have happened for you.

Above in the sky, beyond the range of sight, a ship of the rebel alliance bearing the Princess Leia Organa has been captured by Imperial forces led by the evil lord, Darth Vader. He suspects that the ship is carrying secret plans to the Death Star, the impregnable Imperial battle station with enough firepower to blow planets to smithereens and to assert absolute control over all life in the galaxy.

Knowing that the ship has been captured, Princess Leia loads the stolen plans into the feisty fireplug-shaped robot R2-D2, who, with his companion, the fussy, metallic humanoid robot C-3PO, climbs into an escape pod and slips away to the planet below.

When the robots, or droids as they are called, come into the possession of Luke's uncle, you, as Luke, offer to clean the little droid. You discover that Artoo is carrying in his memory a hologrammatic cry for help from a fetching young woman: "Help me, Obi-Wan Kenobi. You're our only hope."

The repeating message drums into your consciousness, and you watch the girl in a state of fascination. Her beauty awakens in you a yearning for something very familiar and long forgotten. Now that you have seen her, nothing will be the same.

135

When Artoo takes off on his own to deliver the message to the man he says is his rightful owner, you and Threepio set off in your speeder car to retrieve him from old Ben Kenobi, a hermit who some say is crazy, living on the fringe of the dune sea.

Ben Kenobi turns out to be much more than crazy. You are drawn instantly to his wise presence and quiet strength. Clearly the waters run very deep here, and you have the sense that he knows so much more than he is telling you.

You learn that Ben is the last of the legendary society of Jedi knights who defended the freedom of the galaxy but were all but destroyed by the dark forces of the Empire. He tells you that he has a gift for you from your father, an elegant weapon, a saber of light, used by the mysterious order of Jedi knights of which your father, too, was a member.

136

When Artoo plays the whole message for you and Ben, the lovely young woman is identified as Princess Leia. She begs Kenobi to deliver the droid and its stolen plans to her father on Alderaan, who may be able to use them to mount an attack against the Death Star.

"You must come with me to Alderaan," Kenobi tells you. You are sorely tempted, but your old pattern of obedience to the norm and your uncle's wishes is still too strong.

"I can't. I've got to get home."

But there is no home for you to return to. The Imperial Forces have tracked the escaped droids to your uncle's farm. All is in ruins. Everyone is dead. Your bridges have been burned in the most awful way. Destruction has come from the sky, and, like it or not, your adventure has begun.

The Call to Adventure, for this is what Luke experiences when he hears Leia's message, can come in many forms. We generally are called when we find we are living in an outmoded condition, when nothing that we do works, when we have outgrown the comfort zone and feel that our true home lies elsewhere.

However, the Call does not need to be so violent as it was for Luke. It can also come in quiet ways, as a voice clamoring from within or as a whisper of new possibility. But however it comes, it requires immediate action.

For the young prince Gautama Buddha, who has been sheltered by his father from every unpleasant experience, the Call comes when he asks his charioteer to drive him through the town beyond the palace walls. He sees for the first time an old man, a sick man, and a corpse. Unbearably moved by these sights, Gautama vows to leave his home and to search for a way to end human suffering.

How has the Call come for you? Was it a quiet nudge, a loud yoo-hoo, a devastation of the life you had known, or simply a rising of your spirit to open the doors and windows to another way of being?

Or perhaps you feel you are still waiting for the Call, and, regardless of your age, you're still wondering what you're going to be when you grow up.

For the sake of the adventure, let's see what the Call might sound like for you today. Follow the Friend, who leads you to an empty room with dazzling white floor, walls, and ceiling. On a white pedestal, a single black telephone is sitting.

"What is this place?" you ask the Friend.

"It is known as the Call Station," the Friend answers. "Here you receive the Call to the core of your being. This Call will not suggest a solution to your everyday problems. It will not tell you to sell your house, change jobs, or find a new mate. It is a Call that challenges you to wake up to a higher destiny."

Suddenly the phone begins to ring.

At first you are reluctant, perhaps a little afraid, but the ring is insistent.

You pick it up, put it to your ear, and listen for a Call that is uniquely yours. The message may come as words, as images, or even as a strong feeling or hunch. Do not be afraid to ask questions, to engage in dialogue with the Caller. If you wish to make notes of what you hear or to draw a picture of the message, please do so.

Take a moment to reflect on what you have learned in this moment. If you are not sure what the Call means or if no impressions come, know that you can always come back to this place and answer the Call when it comes.

Once you have been called to adventure, you will need some Allies. The journey of transformation is arduous and needs a rich collection of minds and skills to be successful. In traditional stories, the hero's or heroine's Allies are often animals, members of other species, fairy godmothers, magical helpers.

In *The Wizard of Oz,* Dorothy encounters three such Allies: representatives of the vegetable kingdom, the Scarecrow; the mineral kingdom, the Tin Man; and the animal kingdom, the Lion. Together with Dorothy, they follow the Call down the yellow brick road to adventure and discover that the qualities they thought they lacked, they actually had in abundance.

Who will be Luke Skywalker's Allies?

As Luke, you go with your new friends Obi-Wan Kenobi and the two droids to a cantina in the seedy spaceport town of Mos Eisley, where the members of many worlds and many species gather to drink.

There you find the Allies that you are seeking—the cocky, intrepid space jockey, Han Solo, and his companion, the eight-foot furry Wookiee, Chewbacca. Their ship, the Millennium Falcon, will be the vehicle that carries you off the planet and into a larger life.

In Han Solo you meet your opposite. Where you are full of doubts, he is full of certainty. Where you are introverted and naive, he is the complete extrovert, the jaded traveler who has seen and done everything. He is the sun to your moon, the merry Sir Gawain to your dour Sir Percival.

As in all heroic journeys, the Threshold to the Realm of Amplified Power is guarded by fierce forces. For you the guardians at the gate are the white-masked storm troopers of the Empire, who shoot at you and try to keep the Falcon from leaving.

You blast off, only to find Imperial Star Destroyers hovering above the planet. But they are no match for the wild and whimsical piloting of Han Solo, who in spite of impossible odds maintains a jolly, devil-may-care insouciance. This quality of mind, just as much as his ingenious piloting, fools and flusters the stolid and faceless forces that guard the threshold into space.

Outrunning and outgunning the guardian, you cross the threshold at last by making the jump to hyperspace, millions of stars whizzing past, as you are hurled to another part of the galaxy.

The Threshold Guardian is a monster who guards the gateway to the larger reality we seek. In virtually all myths, one is required to prove oneself faster, wiser, and more ingenious than the Guardian in order to make safe passage.

The Guardian is a creature of fixed habits and attitudes. It has a narrow and insular view of its place in the world, and little can be done to budge it. It blocks our path by turning us into a witless version of itself, destroying our moral and spiritual fiber, or even swallowing us whole.

Perhaps the most famous Threshold Guardian is the Cyclops in Homer's *Odyssey.* A cruel giant, he swallows six of Odysseus's men for dinner and is vanquished only when Odysseus uses his wits to get him drunk and pokes out his single eye with a sharpened stick. Then Odysseus and his remaining men make their escape by clinging to the bellies of the monster's sheep as they make their way out of the cave to pasture.

In our own lives, the Guardian can show up as our boss, our church, our parents, our place in society, or even our timeworn habits. In its most subtle and devious form, it

140

manifests as a characteristic mood or emotional quality that colors our consciousness, blocking our access to a larger palate of emotional possibilities.

How often in our lives have we been under the rule of the Monster of Melancholy, the Demon of Doubt, the Dark Angel of Apathy? The Threshold Guardian provides the great testing ground for our character and what we may yet be.

Let us now practice defeating these guardians by doing a most literal exercise.

Somewhere in the middle of the floor, create a threshold. You can do this by setting down small candles at intervals or by laying down a scarf or a piece of string—however you wish to mark the great divide between here and the greater there.

Now choose several representations for what have been or currently are the chief Guardians of your Threshold. For instance, you may lay down along the line photographs of people who you feel have blocked your greater becoming. A symbol of an institution that limits your potential and keeps your spirit from soaring. Cigarettes, chocolate pie, or other things that symbolize habits or addictions that hold you back.

Now step up to the threshold and approach one of the Guardians of your gate. Draw upon the Han Solo aspect of your nature, so that regardless of how fierce this particular Guardian may seem, you maintain the comic edge.

Speak to the Guardian in a cocky, playful way. Engage it in humorous conversation. Confront it in ways it has been never been met by you before. Dance, tell jokes, make fun of it. Tell it why you're much more interesting than it is. Tell it that no matter what, you're moving through.

As you feel the power of this Guardian fade, cross the threshold. Then return to confront another of the Guardians.

For this next Guardian, you may need to use similar skills or do something quite different. You may need to stare it down. Tell it what a dope it is. Lecture it on its own greater possibilities. Turn it into an Ally.

Return across the threshold and repeat the process as often as you need.

Once across, celebrate your passage in some wacky way, worthy of Han Solo. Do a somersault. Put up a sign that says "Good for you!" Throw a party for yourself, inviting your spiritual Allies of the inner world. Treat them to delicious food, thank-you gifts, and dancing.

Celebrating your entrance into the Realm of Amplified Power assures that your passage does not go unremarked by your consciousness.

Once across the threshold into space, you as Luke are trained by Obi-Wan Kenobi in the use of the light saber against an automated target. At first you try consciously to out-think its movements, but you have little success. The target is simply too fast and too devious.

Kenobi tells you that you can succeed only by using the Force, the universal energy field that flows through all things, a tingling aliveness that connects you to all life. When experienced directly, the Force gives you access to a whole new range of potentials. To demonstrate, Kenobi lowers the visor of your helmet so that you cannot see the target.

At first you are doubtful. "How can I see to fight?" you ask, bewildered.

"Your eyes can deceive you, Luke. Don't trust them. Stretch out with your feelings," Kenobi tells you.

You begin to enter a state in which you are deeply relaxed. Your usual thinking process is suspended. You are free, not just in your mind, but in a larger field of being. Everything is known for where it is and what it is, for everything is part of you.

The target approaches. With extraordinary speed, you parry and score a strike. You discover that you have used skill beyond your senses—powers that might be called the rest of your mind. Inner abilities have risen out of the dormant place where they had been hidden.

Within the great enclosure of the Millennium Falcon, you have begun your gestation into higher powers.

143

In this episode, Luke enters the stage of the hero's journey called traditionally the Belly of the Whale. This is a learning time in which one finds oneself swallowed or held within a womblike place to rethink one's purpose and powers.

Jonah in the whale, Hiawatha swallowed by Mishe-Nahma, King of Fishes, Red Riding Hood in the stomach

of the wolf, Jesus in the tomb from which he will be res-
urrected, Osiris sealed into a sarcophagus and cast into
the Nile—the Belly of gestation is the place where we
engage subtle capacities that grant us a new body and a
new mind.

On our life journey, we all experience the Belly of the
Whale in different forms. For some it may be a time of
homebound life, as when we're raising young children or
caring for an ill or elderly family member. For others it can
be a period of isolation, when our family or friends are busy,
preoccupied, or otherwise not available. It can also manifest
as a time of spiritual retreat or deep psychological work,
when our focus is on our own internal processes.

However it manifests, the Belly of the Whale is a powerful time, when we know we must grow or die. If we ignore
or avoid this time of growth, we may fall into a period of
depression or toxic self-doubt. If we say yes to it, our time in
the Belly is time when we go inward, take inventory, and
become aware of a Force within ourselves that links our life
to Great Life.

We drop some of our habits and conditions, even our
ordinary excellence, and agree to a shift in consciousness.
We may come to regard our previous self as a kind of fetus
gestating in the womb of preparatory time for its birth into
a richer life.

Here is a literal way to practice such a shift in consciousness. Luke Skywalker needed to forego actual sight to train
himself to experience the Force within him. You might try a
similar technique yourself.

Find a place where you can go out into nature safely—a garden or wooded park would be ideal. You could also try this exercise indoors, but choose a space that contains plants or other natural objects.

With your eyes closed or actually blindfolded, move around the space, stretching out with your feelings to sense the forms and objects around you.

At first you may bump into things. When you do, stop moving and stop thinking. Hold out your hands, palm to palm, about half an inch apart. Sense the flow of life between them.

With your sense of the Force enhanced, continue to move through the space, stretching out with your feelings to sense the vitality that is within and between all objects. Try to intuit boundaries and edges, stopping before you actually run into things.

Feel yourself to be part of the living flow of vital life that is between you and the tree or rock or plant, you and the bookcase or chair.

Then open your eyes and move through the same space with your eyes open, trying to keep the same sense of the flow of Life Force between you and the objects in the space. Then close your eyes and move again without seeing. Alternate between eyes open and eyes closed until you have a sustained sense of the vital streaming of life energies.

Then practice trying to sense this Force in your everyday life. Become aware of it on the bus, at dinner with your family, or even in church. In this way, you may come

145

to know and feel the ordinary for what it is—manifestations of the extraordinary life that flows through all things.

The scene changes to the Death Star, where Princess Leia watches in horror as Darth Vader and his minion, Governor Tarkin, destroy her home planet of Alderaan because she will not reveal the true location of the rebel base.

Arriving in the area where Alderaan once was, you and the other travelers on the Millennium Falcon find yourself in a sea of rocks, the debris of the destroyed planet.

Your ship is caught in a tractor beam that sucks you into what looks to be a moon but turns out to be the vast machine of the Death Star, the center of operations for the Empire.

146

Now the Road of Trials begins in earnest. Kenobi leaves you with Han and goes off alone to try to release the tractor beam so you can get away. Plugging into the main computer, Artoo discovers that Princess Leia is imprisoned in the Imperial detention block and is scheduled to be executed. Dragging along a reluctant Solo, you go to rescue the princess.

Unlike the typical princess of fairy stories, Leia is feisty, self-directed, and flippantly unafraid. When the Imperial forces are alerted to the rescue, she guides you and Han down a chute into the trash compactor, a terrifying place where you are pulled down beneath the foul waters by a huge creature. Nearly drowning, you pop to the surface at the last moment, as the walls of the compactor begin to close in. Near-death experiences always abound on the Road of Trials.

You escape crushing only barely, when Threepio gets Artoo to shut down the compactors. Artoo releases the hatch and you are free, only to find that you have to fight your way past legions of storm troopers. You engage in high heroics, including swinging on a rope across a vast abyss to safety, carrying the princess in your arms.

As you near the ship, you are transfixed by the sight of Obi-Wan Kenobi, having successfully released the tractor beam, locked in mortal battle with his former student Darth Vader, whose weapon is also a light saber.

When Kenobi sees that you and your friends are safe, he issues a final warning to Vader: "You cannot win, Darth. Strike me down, and I will become more powerful than you can possibly imagine."

With a half-smile, Kenobi puts up his light saber in salute and discorporates, a half-second before Vader slices through his empty robe. Thus Kenobi enters consciously into an extended reality, from where he is able to give you spiritual counsel.

This counsel becomes most useful in your final trial. After winning a furious space battle and delivering the princess and the secret plans to the rebel forces, you suit up to take part in a rebel assault against the Death Star. The odds are impossible—the full force of the Empire ranged against a few brave pilots. Han Solo has disappointed you by refusing to join the final battle.

There seems to be no hope of winning. One by one the rebel ships are shot out of the sky by the omnipresent fighters of the Empire. At last it is only you zooming down the narrow trench that leads to your tiny target, the only hope of destroying the

147

Death Star. Darth Vader is in hot pursuit. Your escort peels off, but Vader's ship stays on your tail.

You switch on your targeting computer and prepare to make your final run. Suddenly you hear a voice. It is unmistakably that of Obi-Wan Kenobi, who tells you, "Use the Force. Let go, Luke. Trust me." You push the targeting screen away, enter into the flow of the Force, and move the controls by instinct.

As you close in on the target, Darth Vader locks you into his sights. It looks like you are finished, but out of the sky comes rescue. It's Han Solo, who blasts Vader off your tail and gives you time to get the shot away. Down the tube it goes.

"Great shot, kid. That was one in a million," Solo exults.

Space fills with fragments, as the Death Star explodes in a spectacular conflagration of evil.

For now, your Road of Trials has come to an end.

148

Through all world literature, the Road of Trials gives the writer ample scope to create hair-raising ordeals and miraculous tests. The hero or heroine enters an unbounded, fluid landscape, symbolic perhaps of the dread that we feel before the unknown and unexplored regions of ourselves—be it desert, wilderness, sea, or outer space.

One is thrust into a series of challenges for which one has had little preparation. Somehow one finds the physical, mental, emotional, and spiritual resources, not just to survive, but to triumph.

One of the most famous classical examples of this stage of the journey is the story of Psyche. Her jealous mother-in-law, Venus, sets Psyche a series of impossible tasks. In one, Psyche must sort before nightfall a huge quantity of various seeds mixed together in a heap. In others, she must gather the golden wool of killer sheep, bottle water from a spring high up on an mountain guarded by dragons, and descend to the Underworld to bring back a box of immortal beauty.

To accomplish each of these tasks, Psyche is helped by some aspect of herself, depicted mythically as an external helper. An army of ants, representing instinct, helps her sort the seeds. A green reed, representing the unconscious, instructs her to gather the wool at night from bushes near where the sheep had grazed. An eagle, representing her spiritual powers, brings her water from the spring. And a tower, representing the collective wisdom of humanity, gives her advice on entering and exiting the Underworld safely.

In a world in which the unexpected is always around the corner—illness, divorce, corporate downsizing, the inevitable stresses of modern life—the Road of Trials is an inevitable part of our life journey.

With preparation, we can meet such challenges as an adventure, not as a wounding unto death. When we are able to do so, we restore the heroic cast of mind to situations that may be less dramatic than Luke Skywalker's but nonetheless critical.

In many myths, the lesson of the Road of Trials is that you have forces within yourself that will allow you to see your way through tests and challenges, regardless of their level of difficulty. Trusting these forces is the key.

To practice this skill, let's see what we can learn from the four labors of Psyche, as they constitute in symbolic form the major tasks of our life. Accomplishing these trials as acts of imagination may create the energy that will allow you to be similarly heroic in everyday life.

The first challenge is Sorting the Seeds. In our lives, this might mean sorting out the jumbled details of ordinary life. It may involve making lists of tasks you need to do, but it can also mean cleaning out your desk or closet, balancing your checkbook, paying taxes, answering letters, or even setting new priorities that give you sacred time for quiet reflection, spiritual exercise, or entertainment.

For the purpose of this exercise, choose the sorting task that seems necessary for you. In your imagination, visualize yourself actually performing this task. Go through the motions physically, as a sort of rehearsal, so that the pattern is embedded in your mind.

Then make time to actually do the task. Regard your labor as a heroic exercise—an adventure on the Road of Trials—and celebrate your successful accomplishment.

Psyche's second task is Gathering the Golden Fleece. You might think of the Golden Fleece as representing whatever career or form of employment will result in your appropriate abundance.

Your task in this labor is to use your intuition, your green reed into the unconscious, to see a way to make your job into what the Buddhists call "right livelihood"—a means of earning a living that contributes to your and the world's spiritual and social evolution.

Consider your job, whether it is at home or in an office or school, as standing for the Golden Fleece. Look at it from afar, as if it were on the opposite bank of a river. Regard it in the broad daylight of consciousness, seeing all its flaws and dangers as well as its virtues and possibilities.

Now, listening to the reed of your own intuitive wisdom, look at it again as if in the dark of the moon, when you can see what is really valuable about it that has been left out of your thinking.

Ask yourself: Who is served or helped by what I do? How could this service be perfected or enhanced? What would I need to do to make my job a joy and a pleasure rather than an unpleasant task?

Make notes of what the reed of intuition tells you. You may come to know that you should make a deeper personal connection to your co-workers or offer help and emotional support to new employees. You may see new possibilities for projects, new ways of reaching out into the community, new ways to make your work reflect your values.

Make a conscious and heroic effort to implement whatever ideas you receive.

Psyche's third task is fetching the Waters of Life. We might think of the Waters of Life as symbolizing greater vitality and energy for all the tasks we must do. As more and more people are coming to realize, the world's spiritual traditions—like Psyche's eagle—teach many ways of gaining access to the vital energies of the mind-body system. One of the most effective is visualization and focused breathing.

To begin, focus on the base of your spine and have a sense of inhaling deeply up from the base of the spine and along it to the top of your head. When you reach the top of your head, continue to inhale, imagining that above your head is a pool containing the restorative Waters of Life. Gather these waters with your breath.

Now, as you exhale, have a sense of bringing the Waters of Life down the front of your body, allowing them to bathe and fill every nerve and sinew, every nook and cranny, every cell and organ, restoring and replenishing your vital spirits as they do so.

Repeat the process, again breathing up your spine and tapping into the Waters of Your Life. Exhale down the front, bringing these waters into your body, the vehicle that carries your soul and spirit in this time.

Continue to do this as a focused meditation for about ten minutes, aware of the ascension of the breath, the gaining of the Waters of Life, and their absorption into the body-mind system with each exhalation.

Don't go on automatic. Focus and awareness is everything.

After ten minutes, stretch and walk around a bit and notice how much more vital and alive you may be feeling.

Psyche's fourth labor is the descent into the Underworld. For us, the Underworld may represent the deep inward time we need to do our human spiritual and psychological homework.

In the story of Psyche, the Tower, which represents the collective wisdom of culture and civilization, warns her to

152

curb her constant availability to others. In our lives, we may need to practice saying no to the demands of others in order to give ourselves time and space to do our inner work—to delve into our Underworld and bring back its treasures.

This part of the Road of Trials is one of the most difficult challenges we face. When we put all our energy into external tasks and concerns, we have little time to dive deep and make waves in the inner worlds of psyche and spirit.

One way to accomplish this task is to write a covenant with yourself. Take a beautiful piece of paper and actually write a covenant. You might write, for instance:

"I (name) do solemnly promise my Higher Self to spend (blank) minutes each day living at a deeper level than my ordinary world and consciousness, there to give time and place to the practice and development of my deepest beauty."

153

As Luke, you now know that your Higher Parent, Obi-Wan Kenobi, will always be with you. What remains is to enter the deepest part of the mythological realm where you meet the Goddess or heavenly partner and are given the boon, the insight or the recognition necessary for you to take your learnings back into the world.

In Star Wars, recognition occurs for you gloriously. Amid the green trees of a flourishing planet, you, Han, and Chewie enter the spiritual center of the Rebel Alliance. The stone walls are decked with luxurious vines, suggesting that you have entered the green world that will redeem the gray wasteland of the Empire, for don't doubt that your adventures will continue.

Here, however, there is a respite. With pride and splendor, you move forward past the applauding citizens of the Alliance to meet the Goddess in the form of Princess Leia at her most radiant. Behind her is a luminous art deco cathedral of light.

She places around your neck and those of your fellows a great boon, medallions of honor. As you look at her, you know you have met your heavenly partner. In fact, as you will discover, she is your twin sister. By your side, Han Solo winks at her, and you intuit that one day they will become earthly partners.

But for now in this numinous moment you have come into your own, a greater being by far than the boy you were when you began this journey. Everybody recognizes it, and, more important, you know it as well.

Eventually you and your friends will return to fight further battles. You will gain higher training from the great teacher of the Jedi, the elfin master Yoda, meet new Allies, and even restore the light of goodness to your human father, Darth Vader.

By bringing the light out of what had been his darkness, you will become the Master of Two Worlds—the mythic realm of the Force and the ordinary realm of space and time. You will be a force for the Force, returning the ancient wisdom into once and future times long, long ago in a galaxy far, far away.

This is a time for celebration. The journey has been taken, the obstacles are overcome, your knowledge and willingness to serve have brought you to the Temple of the Heart, the place from which the greening of your world will proceed.

But first you must acknowledge and be acknowledged by the one who is known as the Beloved or Heavenly Partner. This glorious being is your other half, who dwells in the depth world, the Godself from whom you are now able and willing to receive the gift of full recognition.

When you are known for who and what you are, you will be able to know others and recognize the Godself in them.

With the Force moving strongly within you, sense now the Divine Other. Go out in the evening or early morning, when Venus is bright in the sky, and using that planet of love as the symbol of the Beloved, say words such as these:

"From this moment forth I am with you always. From this moment forward, I am your partner in the human realm. From this moment forward, I will bring you, my Beloved, and your ways into time. I know you will ignite the fire in my mind and bathe me in the love that passes understanding. As it was in the beginning, now, and ever shall be, love and life without end."

Now you have gifts to give because you have received so much. Perhaps you should give a party for friends that you wish to acknowledge and empower. At this party, celebrate each guest publicly, speaking to each powerfully from the wisdom of your heart about their true worth and quality. Don't dwell on negatives, but rather celebrate their growth and their own unique soul journey.

Like the Wizard at the end of the Oz story, give each one a small present that in some way symbolizes how deeply you see and acknowledge them.

155

For instance, for someone who has overcome illness, you might give a certificate for a massage or a free visit to a health club. For another who has bought a new house, give a miniature house, which everyone present blesses. For one who has entered into a new love relationship, give a woven scarf that symbolizes the ties that bind. And for one who is making a new beginning, give a block of clay symbolizing the freedom to shape a new life. Make sure that there is music and plenty of good food.

The Friend asks you to stand back now and look at where you have traveled as Luke. You have moved through the perils of adolescence to adulthood. You have come into your powers and become in truth a Jedi, like your father. You faced the enormous challenges of the Road of Trials and discovered the use of your full intelligence, the opening of your heart, friendship and compassion, and the courage that comes of taking risks and meeting challenges.

You also learned about the genius of community and how the small committed band can do almost anything. "Never doubt," said that Jedi taskmaster Margaret Mead, "that a small group of thoughtful committed citizens can change the world. Indeed, it is the only thing that ever has."

Finally, you have learned about the Force, the sacred potency that is within each of us.

You have returned a mythic being and, like Luke, you now have the chance to green the wasteland of your own particular Empire with your newfound knowings.

156

Now you are ready to leave the Realm of Myth, and so you do, passing the carved door of many symbols and stories.

Moving rapidly up and around the interior mountain, you glance at the mirrored door of the Realm of the Psyche. How interesting! You see reflected in it the droids, Han and Chewie, Leia, and even your healed father, Yoda, and Obi-Wan Kenobi, bathed in shimmering blue light. They wave at you, and you wave and salute in farewell.

Then, traveling upward, you pass the gorgeous door to the Realm of the Senses. A hand reaches out to offer you a ripe delicious apple, a symbol of the new knowledge you have won.

Finally, reaching the top, you climb out and make your way down the mountain, where you take stock of the new powers and gifts you have gained on your heroic journey.

May the Force always be with you!

157

❧ THE SPIRITUAL QUEST

> If I am to know God directly, I must become completely God, and God I, so that this God and this I become one I.
>
> MEISTER ECKHART

Wandering the Earth as I do, I eventually run into everybody. And almost everybody I meet seem to be on a spiritual quest or experiencing a growing hunger for it. The hound of heaven woofs at their heels, urging them to wake up to their spiritual possibilities.

The thing about everybody is that they try everything. For sheer creativity and inventiveness, nothing beats spiritual adventuring.

People meditate or fast or pray in search of Divine connection. They make outlandish promises—giving up sex, calories, comfort. They go mad or go manic, become zealots, hush their minds into quiescence and empty themselves of thought, hoping to tempt God to fill the void.

They walk on burning coals, sit in the snow, count their breaths, twirl into ecstasy, make pilgrimages to places where God or His/Her local incarnations are reputed to have placed their feet. They try out religions as different as possible from the ones in which they were raised, go on spiritual shopping sprees, twist their bodies into uncomfortable positions, change their names.

Mostly, they shout at God, begging the Great One to finally show up in their lives.

I'm not criticizing these practices; I've tried them all. And don't laugh—so have you, perhaps in other ways.

There are many signs that point to your being on a spiritual quest, even if you have not named it as such:

Do you wonder every time you pass a book counter if truth is to be found on its shelves today?

How many books have you bought this year that have *soul* in the title?

Are you always heading off to a seminar or a church retreat?

Is your house filled with angel images—cards, statues, books, candles?

Do you have an acupuncturist, a massage therapist, a medicine cabinet full of supplements?

When you get the flu, do you take vitamins and echinacea instead of standard-brand antibiotics?

Do you frequent health-food stores?

Have you thought about trying to be a vegetarian?

Have you quit the softball league and signed up for a class in yoga or tai chi?

Are you surfing the internet?

Do you find yourself hiding what you're reading when your relatives enter the room, even though it's not the least bit sexy?

Have you divorced a spouse because he or she just wasn't on the same wavelength?

Do your kids think you are weird?

Do your CDs thrum with chants and drums and Celtic harps?

Are you a fan of TV shows about mythic heroes, outer space, immortals, parapsychology?

Are you sometimes unaccountably surprised by joy?

Are you reading this book?

If you have answered yes to any of the above, chances are you're hooked! As well you might be, for the complexity of the present time seems to demand a deepening of our nature if we are going to survive. Deepening requires exploration. And for all its byways, exploration leads ultimately to the spiritual source of our existence.

Not since the days of Plato and Buddha and Confucius, some 2500 years ago, has there been such an uprising of spiritual yearning. Now, as then, the explosion of spirituality is happening on many continents and takes many forms.

Though the varieties of contemporary religious experience may look or sound different, they share a core belief. I often like to end my longer seminars by playing a game that demonstrates this commonality. It's called "Are You God in Hiding?"

I ask all in the room to close their eyes and move around until, naturally, they bump into someone. Then they ask that person, "Are you God in hiding?"

The person being asked responds with the same question, "Are you God in hiding?"

Players keep on for several minutes, asking the same question and getting the same answer.

But one person, whom I designate after all everyone has closed their eyes by placing my hand strongly on his or her head, *is* "God in Hiding."

When someone comes up to this person and asks "Are you God in hiding?" this person remains silent. By this silence, the person asking the question becomes "godded," too, and remains silent.

In a short time, the entire room becomes absolutely quiet. I have seen five hundred people go from a buzz of excited conversation to absolute silence in less than a minute—that's how quickly "godding" travels.

After the silence has deepened, I say, "Now open your eyes and look at all the gods no longer in hiding."

Eyes open simultaneously all over the room. People look at one another. First there is a hush, then a gasp of wonder and astonishment. Recognition pervades the room. Eyes shine. Laughter begins. People embrace. For a few moments people drop their brain cataracts and see the truth about one another.

This simple but telling game—a God game, if you will—draws on a tradition found in every spiritual path—Judaism, Islam, Christianity, Buddhism, Hinduism, as well as the beliefs of indigenous peoples.

162

Though expressed in different words, the tradition holds that each human being contains a Godseed, a divine essence that can be nurtured through spiritual practice into a fully matured expression of the God stuff within.

The recommended practices to grow this Godseed vary from culture to culture and from person to person—yoga, meditation, contemplative prayer, mindfulness, as well as the various explorations into God mentioned above.

But all paths seem to agree that in addition to inwardly directed practices, spiritual growth also requires simple acts of compassion and service based on the recognition of the divine presence in all beings and the wish to serve the God in one another.

A famous Buddhist painting of heaven and hell illustrates why serving others matters. In hell, people are sitting at a banquet of magnificent foods with spoons so long they can never reach their mouths. In heaven, people are sitting at the same kind of banquet, using the long spoons to feed one another.

Moreover, belief in a divine essence as the basis of reality is not limited to explicitly religious paths. Scientists of a spiritual bent explain reality in terms that are not much different from those mystics use.

While mystics speak of steps on the path to union with the Infinite, scientist-seekers talk about the frequency bands of consciousness, some of which are closer than others to Universal Being.

Speculative scientists often use the metaphor of the hologram to explain humanity's place in the Universal Mind. Each part of a hologram contains an image of the whole. Break up a hologram image, shine a special kind of laser light though any of its pieces, and you get the whole picture back again.

In spiritual terms, we might think of ourselves as fragments of the great hologram of Reality. Shine the proper light of consciousness through us, and we each reflect the whole—starfish and sequoias and a mountain goat leaping about in the Pyrenees.

That letter you never wrote to your grandma and a ball of twine rolling in the cabin of a boat in Bangkok.

Other galaxies and the child who is just now discovering that she can read.

Horses running on an Arabian shore and the joke you heard the other night.

163

The sap rising in the winter trees and the yearning of God for each of us . . .

That's all very well and good, you may be saying at this point, but how does all this relate to me? I've never in my life reflected the whole, much less horses running on an Arabian shore! I just want to know who and what I really am, that's all.

This yearning to know our true nature is universal. We're all a bit like the philosophy student who goes to his professor's office. His eyes are red rimmed with exhaustion, his brow puckered with worrisome thought. Trembling and angst ridden, he approaches his gray-haired mentor, "Please sir, I've got a question that's eating me alive. I've got to know! Sir, do I exist?"

The professor turns to him with a withering look and replies, "Who wants to know?"

We recall that Saint Francis stated the problem in a similar way when describing the goal of the spiritual quest: "What we are looking for," he said, "is who is looking."

Discovering who is looking is what life is ultimately all about. If the mystics are to be believed, the answer is itself a riddle that points to the Infinite Answer. The medieval mystical writer Meister Eckhart has God speak to us saying: "I became man for you. If you do not become God for me, you do me wrong."

To help us bridge the great divide in consciousness between the divine self and our limited local, try for a moment to imagine how it might be to experience reality from the divine point of view.

What would we perceive if we could magically switch perspective and be EVERYTHING experiencing ourselves, rather than the other way around?

Would we be filled with the knowledge that our local mind is but a focusing down of universal consciousness?

Would we know absolutely that the ground underlying our finite human self is the infinite divine Self, the Great WHO bubbling Itself up in an interesting corner of space and time, mind and body, called Robert or Margaret or Jean or Frank?

Very young children seem to know this secret in their own way:

"Where did you come from, baby dear?"

"Out of everywhere into here."

Like children, spiritual questers through the centuries have always suspected that Self-ing is something Infinity does for fun. Underlying the finite human self, they have taught in their various ways, is an infinite Consciousness, a Great Who, experiencing Itself through the mind and body of that bubbling up of Being in space and time called You!

And what is more important, the Godself within is a natural birthright that comes with being human. "Closer than breathing, nearer than hands and feet," say the scriptures about the presence of the divine in our lives.

If we could only know this absolutely for a minute, drop our boundaries, release our brain cataracts, it would be like waking up from a dream.

There would be a powerful clarity and vitality to everything—people, trees, rocks, jet planes, our own body.

All of these would seem related to one another so perfectly that we would know that we are in the presence of an artistic masterpiece.

We would feel overwhelming appreciation of the simple ordinariness of things—a child's freckles, washing dishes, the sound of milk pouring into a glass.

When I have studied or talked with seekers who have had this experience, they have told me of a joy that passes understanding, an immense surge of creativity, a instant uprush of kindness and tolerance that make them impassioned champions for the betterment of all, bridge builders, magnets for solutions, peacemakers, pathfinders.

Best of all, other people feel enriched and nourished around them. Everyone they touch becomes more, because they themselves are more.

How can we birth this miracle within ourselves? How can we foster our natural birthright of spiritual presence? What keeps us from mystical knowing?

Let me tell you about cataracts. I recently had a cataract removed from my left eye—my first and only operation. Going from seeing through a cloudy glass very darkly to seeing pretty well got me thinking about the cataracts that cloud all human vision.

The poet says that our birth is but a forgetting of heaven, which is our home. Having seen the seraphic smiles on the faces of babies, I don't think they have forgotten much.

Nonetheless, as we grow, so do our cataracts. School, siblings, society gradually seem to thicken the luminous lens we each have embedded in us for God-centered knowing.

166

Pathologies spring up around this thickened lens—mental and emotional delusions, disappointment with life, adulthood's inevitable neuroses. As life progresses, more and more we lose awareness of the Infinite Self's appetite for wonder and delight.

Yet somehow we can remember. That is what has brought you to this book—an effort to remember. You have traveled far in working with levels of the self, learning practices that can dissolve the cataracts clouding remembrance.

In the Realm of the Senses you opened new doors of perception. In the Realm of the Psyche you discovered your soul's partners who can connect you with greater creativity and the mastery of skills. In the Realm of Myth and Symbol you quested for a clearer vision of your life through the transforming adventures of the hero's journey.

Each realm helped wear away the habits of consciousness that sustain the brain's cataracts. As you continue to work in these levels, you will lose many more cataracts still.

But now we have reached the final threshold. Our challenge here is to learn to live so as to avoid further cataracts and to come back to who we really are.

For the richest experience of what is to come, please have a plant or a vase of flowers nearby, as well as a recording of some rhythmic music to dance to, preferably with drums and a strong percussive beat. Also have some drawing or painting materials near at hand.

So here you are once more, at the bottom of the mountain, ready to make your final journey. This time the Friend, your Essential Self, joins you early, for this one knows the Way in ways that you or I do not.

You begin the trek up the spiral path, noticing many small things you hadn't seen before. How the rushing water in the brook curls over the rock. The worm on the path, which you pick up and carry over to the side. The blue eggshell from a newly hatched bird.

It seems to be spring, and as the forest gives way to high meadow, a riot of wildflowers surrounds you. Finally, you reach the top, lift off the stone tablet, and enter the mountain. From a long way down comes the sound of rushing water.

168

You make your way quickly down and around the inside of the mountain. Passing the door to the sensory realm, you notice set within it a small fountain issuing cool, clear water. You drink and feel strangely energized, as if you were awakening from a long sleep.

Moving down and around, you come to the mirrored entrance to the psychological realm. Now it reflects only your face and body as they are now. Somehow this image gives you considerable satisfaction.

Continuing down the path, you reach the entrance to the mythic level. This time the wooden door is perfectly smooth, no carvings, no symbols. Its blank surface is waiting for the imprint of a new story—your story.

Now the path becomes much steeper, the sound of a waterfall becoming ever louder. Finally you reach it, a shining sheet of water, the entrance to the Realm of the Spirit.

As you and your Friend pass beneath the falls, you feel a drenching that is a cleansing of your entire being. The regrets and sorrows of your life seem to be washed away, and your mind is as clear and luminous as the dawn sky.

Before you is a vast radiant structure that appears to be a Rose. From where you are standing, you can see its innermost petals as well as the ones near its outer edge. In some traditions, this flower is called the White Rose of the Empyrean. In others, the Rose of Union with the Divine.

"What is this immense Rose?" you ask the Friend. "What does it mean?"

The Friend answers, "The Rose has always been the symbol of beauty and life, love and joy—all the qualities of communion and union with the Divine Beloved. But remember, for all its beauty, every rose is circled by thorns. Often the journey to greater awareness is arduous, painful, strewn with challenges.

"But once you arrive at the place where you are no longer blind to God, you come upon the Rose, the image of the Love that holds the scattered leaves of your life and the life of the universe together."

Now a fragrance rises from the Rose, so sweet, so filled with the essence of everything you care about, that you are drawn to move closer.

Along with the Friend, you slip through an opening in the outermost petal. Within the layers, a pathway winds inward, following the spiral of the Rose's shape.

The tender petals rise around you, white and luminous, vital with life force. Blissful with the beauty of being within the Rose, you find yourself waking up more and more with each step you take.

You hear the sound of many voices singing so beautifully you wonder if it is a choir of angels. Forever would not be too long to stand and listen.

But your Friend urges you onward: "Follow me, and I will introduce you to some Friends of mine."

The Friend goes on to explain that the path leads to places of learning and reflection. Each is presided over by a great teacher who represents one of the varieties of spiritual experience. Each can share a unique perspective on the life of Spirit in time.

As you spiral inward, you are stunned at the rich possibilities of the spiritual life. You recognize some of the teachers instantly and notice that friends of yours are already studying with them.

There are the Buddha and Saint Francis of Assisi, Saint Teresa of Avila and Julian of Norwich. There are Moses and Isaiah, Maimonides, Mahavira, and Confucius. There are Jesus and his mother Mary, Muhammad, William Blake Sojourner Truth, and Dag Hammarskjöld. There is the great Hindu sage Ramakrishna and Madame Blavatsky there, too, an African wise woman famed in her time for her healing gifts.

But the names of many of the teachers that you pass are unknown to you, though you can see that they represent all races and all times. Some seem to belong to Native

American, Australian Aboriginal, and South Pacific peoples, as well as to peoples of Africa and South America. All are deeply engrossed, some merrily so, in imparting wisdom to their students.

The Friend now leads you into a glorious garden within a petal of the Rose. It abounds with flowers and trees and vegetation of every kind. In the center is a fountain from which springs water so sparkling clear it seems to be the water of life itself.

The garden, the Friend explains, is a universal symbol of the spiritual life. In the inner garden, wisdom and understanding bloom as the fruits and flowers of one's soul.

Someone is in this garden—a woman in a medieval nun's habit. She bends over one of the plants, examining it closely. You can hear her singing in a high pure voice:

> *I am the breeze that nurtures all things green.*
> *I encourage blossoms to flourish with ripening fruits.*
> *I am the rain coming from the dew that causes the grasses*
> *to laugh with the joy of life. . . .*

The woman notices you and speaks, in a voice like the song, "Ah, welcome! You have brought your Friend with you. Please, come here, both of you. I want to show you the greening power of life."

As you move toward her, the Friend explains that this is the mystic, scientist, philosopher, poet, prophet, painter, musician, botanist, and lover of nature known in our time as Hildegard of Bingen. In the twelfth century, she was abbess of a convent in Bavaria.

Mother Hildegard hands you a leaf.

"This leaf can cure headache," she tells you, "but see how it also reflects God's wonder. Here in the branching veins of the leaf is the very signature of God. A leaf is a world in miniature, a Tree of All Life.

"Just as the leaf is fed by the greening power in the veins, so all things are fed by patterns of living force. Trees, plants, and minerals, even animals, are sustained by rivers of energy like those in these leaves.

"But God has also created patterns that connect forms of life with one another. God has arranged things so that each part of creation is linked with everything else."

"I can understand how nature is interwoven," you reply, "but as a human being, I often feel separated from all that."

Mother Hildegard nods sadly. Suddenly she brightens and says, "Then let me invite you to feel as I feel, know as I know. I was fortunate. I lived in the lush green Rhine Valley, where the greening of the world and of the soul were everywhere apparent. Perhaps I can show you what I mean. Would you please let me hold your hand for a minute?"

She takes your hand in hers, and you feel the rough strong palm of someone who has spent years working in gardens and fields.

In a moment, you begin to feel another kind of energy—soul energy—coursing through you. It is the energy of one who has agreed to be God's eyes, God's senses, God's worker in the world. Weary cataracts slip away, and you see the garden as Mother Hildegard sees it—fresh, unspoiled, newly created.

Mother Hildegard speaks, and you follow her suggestions.

"Child, do you know we are all living branches of God's own body? Feel now the power of refreshment flowing through you, like sap rising in the springtime.

"In order to be a co-worker with God, we must become a flowering orchard. But to flower we must first know our innate creative potential. We are dressed in the scaffold of creation. The very cosmos is embedded in our human form. Be that creation now. Yes, be that creation.

"Stretch your hand out over the garden and say with me, 'I am the fiery life of divine wisdom. I ignite the beauty of the plains. I sparkle the waters. I burn in the sun, the moon, and the stars. I am the blowing wind, the mild, moist air, the exquisite greening of trees and grasses. I adorn the earth. All creation is now called, quickened, awakened by the resounding melody of my word.'

"Speak the word, now."

"'Be!'"

The word *BE* resounds through the garden, echoing and reverberating like the beat of a human heart.

"That, Child, is God knowing," Mother Hildegard says softly.

"Now for human knowing," she continues, "let us take the time to examine this leaf more closely."

173

Inspired by Hildegard's words, look now at the plant or flower you have at hand. Study it from all directions. Gently touch its surfaces, and feel their greening power. Sense how it loves the Earth and lifts itself to worship the sun.

Take your art materials and sketch or paint the plant or flower now—not just its form, but its life force as well. If writing is your medium, describe it in words, writing, perhaps, as if you were the flower itself. As you work, imagine that the plant or flower is communicating with you, helping you to express its essence as best you can. Feel it painting or describing itself through you.

When you have finished, Mother Hildegard speaks again. "Every time, Child, you stop to look closely at nature, give it a blessing. Remember, all creative, all germinating power is within you, for you are of God and of the Earth. The Earth is the Mother of all that is natural, all that is human. Stay juicy. Stay Earthy. Stay green ... and above all, laugh a lot and stay good humored."

Thanking Mother Hildegard, you move on with Friend, continuing along the spiral path deeper into the Rose.

In the distance, you hear drumming, which grows louder as you move deeper into the interior of the flower. Soon you come to its source, an African shaman and spiritual teacher sitting in a jungle clearing, beating out a powerful rhythm on a huge tribal drum.

He is a large man dressed in a flowing, multicolored, striped caftan, a matching cap on his head.

"Isn't he cool?" your Friend asks as you watch in wonder, your body beginning to pulse to the beat.

174

At your puzzled expression at the word *cool,* the Friend explains that among the peoples of West Africa, *cool* refers to that spark of creative or spiritual sophistication that gives a person grace under pressure, royal bearing, artistic brilliance, and high character. Clearly, this man has passionate art and a passionate consciousness.

The drum with its beat is his spiritual teaching. Of all musical instruments, the drum is the most pregnant with mystic ideas. Its beat is the dialogue between matter and Spirit, human consciousness and the rhythm of the natural world. Drumming announces a flash of Spirit, a streaming immensity of the divine voice calling the human soul into greater becoming.

In Africa and other shamanic cultures, the Friend explains, the drum is the instrument of rapture and communion. The drum allows us to "go south" in our psyche, to dissolve the comfortable categories that keep us far away from Spirit's awesome power. As the drumhead of the self throbs and pulses, the great divide between "me" and "not me" is bridged, and the human world and the Spirit world meet in a numinous flow of "cool" ecstasy.

The shaman calls out to you, his voice echoing the drum's cadence. "Come. Dance. Let the rhythm enter your mind. Your body. Your spirit. Soon you will become Spirit. One who does not dance does not know God."

Answering this invitation, dance for a while to the strong rhythmic beat of the music you have ready or, if you prefer, to your hands clapping in accompaniment. As you move, feel the Spirit moving in you. If you stay with the rhythm, after a while you will not know or care where Spirit begins and you leave off, or whether it makes any difference, so filled are you with blessed and joyous rapture.

You begin to understand how the drum can be the key to spiritual encounter and dance its instrument. To meditate in this way is to dance, to let go, to allow the portals of the self to open.

If this path seems right for you, allow yourself some sacred time each day to invite Spirit to join you in the dance. With full awareness of the sacred nature of what you are doing, put on appropriate music and dedicate the dance to communion with Spirit. You may also wish to take up drumming yourself as a way to further this connection.

Leaving the place of the drum, you travel deeper into the Rose, coming eventually to a gate in the shape of a heart.

"Here is the entrance to the path of love," the Friend explains. "Through this gateway you will find the revelation of the heart—the revelation that it is love that brings you closest to God and to creation. Love opens your heart so that the whole world can stream in to be cherished."

Entering the gateway of the heart, you are greeted by an ecstatic bearded man, dressed in wide pants, pointed shoes, and a turban. He embraces you wildly, saying:

There's a strange frenzy in my head,.
of birds flying
each particle circulating on its own.
Is the one I love everywhere?

"Yes, Master Rumi," the Friend replies, "the one you love is everywhere."

The Friend introduces you to Jelaluddin Rumi, the Persian mystic who lived and taught in Turkey in the thirteenth century. His path is that of the heart and his spiritual practice, falling madly in love with the Divine Beloved. "He's written a lot of poetry about this love affair," the Friend explains.

Rumi laughs, spins a bit, demonstrating:

We've given up making a living.
It's all this crazy love poetry now.
It's everywhere. Our eyes and our feelings
focus together, with our words.

"I cannot help myself, friend," Rumi explains. "I am the pawn of my inspiration."

Every hair of mine has become, due to Thy love, verse
and ghazal,
Every limb of mine has become, due to Thy relish, a
barrel of honey.

"What he says is true," your Friend continues. "Master Rumi has composed tens of thousands of verses—quatrains, odes, a kind of Persian poetry called ghazal, and even a vast spiritual epic. Within their honeyed lines is an encyclopedic outpouring, an ecstasy of knowledge.

"Rumi knows the whole as well as the parts. The path of spiritual love has brought him into harmony with the

Pattern That Connects All Life. Through love of the Divine Beloved, his mind and soul have awakened to everything to be known in the inner and outer worlds. The path of love can do the same for you."

"How, then, can I enter this path of the heart?" you ask.

Rumi is only too willing to show you a way to begin. Inviting you to sit with him on a cushion of embroidered silk, he teaches you a practice that Sufis do. They call it a *zikkr*.

"This," Rumi says, "is the zikkr of communion with God, the Beloved.

"Inhale deeply, while thinking of the presence of God as the Beloved of your soul. Then, as you exhale, make three sounds deep in your throat, which arise from the very center of your chest where your heart is. The sound that you make is 'HMMM, HMMM, HMMM.'

"Be aware of the vibration in your chest as you make this sound. Each time it arises, feel a sense of communing with whatever deity or image or idea you understand to be the Spiritual Beloved of your soul. For you who are Christian, it may be union with Christ. For you who are Buddhist, it may be the Buddha Nature.

"Feel and believe that the One who is Love Itself is communing with you, loving you as you do this practice.

"Know also that this deep humming is the ultimate sound. It is the sound of babies at the breast. It is the sound of making love. It is deep and ancient in the brain. It is the sound of waves meeting the shore after their long journey across the ocean.

"Stay very focused as you make the three HMMMs on each breath, remembering that the Beloved yearns for you just as much as you are yearning for the Beloved.

"If you wish to enter upon the practice in the formal Sufi style, sound three HMMMs on each of a cycle of thirty-three outbreaths—ninety-nine soundings of HMMM.

"A good way to complete the practice is to acknowledge the Beloved and give reverence. This you do by bowing from the waist slowly and deeply three times. First to the Beloved who is within you. Then to the Beloved in others. And finally, bowing to the Beloved That Is. Then sit quietly, meditating on your experience."

Inspired by Rumi's potent instruction, try this practice now, breathing in a sense of divine presence and breathing out with three deep soundings of HMMM. Do this several times. When you have come to silence, bow deeply to the Beloved and sit in quiet contemplation of union with the Lover of All.

179

The zikkr of communion is a most powerful practice, because when the sound of the sweetness of union is joined to a sense of the divine presence, it helps block negative habitual patterns and toxic thoughts.

When you get up to leave, you see Rumi in the distance whirling and singing to the Beloved:

My soul spills into yours and is blended.
Because my soul has absorbed your fragrance, I cherish it.

Leaving the place of the heart, you travel further into the Rose, drawn to what appears to be the image of a great open eye. "The open eye," the Friend tells you, "is always associated with awakening. Just as the physical eye is the extension of the brain, so the spiritual eye, often imagined as being in the center of the forehead, is seen as a symbol of spiritual vision.

"In the process of awakening, the physical eye and the inner, spiritual eye become one. This union of inner and outer vision is what Christ meant when he said, 'If therefore thine eye be single, thy whole body shall be full of light.'"

As you come closer, you see that within the eye is an unadorned room, in which a monk in a simple gray robe is sitting perfectly still, staring at a blank, white wall. The Friend tells you that this is the revered Zen master known as Roshi Dogen, who lived in thirteenth-century Japan.

180

"He is known for his abrupt and surprising ways of making a point. Go speak to him now," the Friend urges. "He has finished his meditation."

You approach and bow to Roshi Dogen. He bows back. In a faltering voice, you ask him to share with you his highest teaching.

In response, Roshi Dogen picks up a brush, dips it into a pot of ink, and writes a single word on the white wall: *Attention.*

"Of course," you say, "but surely there is something more?"

Roshi Dogen smiles, nods, picks up the brush once more and writes, *Attention.*

"Come now," you protest, "that can't be all. What else is important?"

Again the Roshi laughs, turns back to the wall, and writes once more, *Attention.*

Now you read the whole message: "Attention. Attention. Attention."

As you have discovered during your visits to other parts of the interior mountain, *attention* means mindfulness to whatever is before you—sensory impressions, memories and emotions, stories. Attention helps you go off automatic pilot and be present to the glory of the moment.

When you first begin to practice mindfulness, you may need to stop yourself many times during the day and remind yourself of Roshi Dogen's teaching, "Attention. Attention. Attention." Gradually mindfulness becomes a habit, and the world and your relationship to it changes.

"I have some idea of how to work on attention in my outer life," you tell Roshi Dogen, "but my mind is so busy, I get lost in my thoughts and feelings. What can I do about that?"

In answer, Roshi Dogen points to the blue sky. Then to a passing cloud. Then back to the blue sky. He indicates with his hand that you should attend to the blue sky. He motions for you to sit by him. When you do, you feel a subtle transmission of his Zen teaching.

For a while, you sit in stillness, in a state of peaceful equanimity, riding the waves of your own breathing. Your sitting posture is dignified and self-contained, like a mountain rising out of the plain or a temple seated majestically in a forest. You are rooted to Earth, while your mind is the sky.

181

Picture, now, your mind as a clear blue sky. As thoughts arise, imagine them to be clouds that pass across the sky of your consciousness. Watch them go, but do not become attached to them or follow them. As they pass away, return once more to a gentle focus on the clarity and purity of the blue, cloudless sky. . . .

As you practice, practice, and continue to practice this simple meditation, you will be building a new body, a new mind. Life's stresses will gradually cease to overwhelm you. Creative possibilities will be greeted with delight. Peace of mind and clarity of spirit will become a way of being.

After bowing to the Roshi in profound thanks for his teaching, you leave the open eye gateway.

Together with the Friend, you walk to a place where deep quiet reigns. There is no sound, no light, no touch, taste, or smell, and yet everything seems primed to bud forth from a deep, dense silence. It seems that you, too, are part of this silence in which everything has come to rest.

When you have rested in the silence for a few moments, a voice wells up from within you, "Let the Great Friend now appear."

Who or what appears in answer to this request, I cannot say, for the appearance of the Great Friend is different for each person. To some it may seem to be an angel. To others, the personification of the Christ Consciousness or the Buddha Nature.

Still others may see the Great Friend in the garb of a classical god or goddess or in one of the forms of the Divine Feminine—Mother Earth, wise Sophia, gracious Kwan

Yin. And it may be that you see nothing at all but experience a sound, a touch, a vibration, a sense of Presence.

However the Great Friend appears to you, remember that this internal spiritual figure is part of you, an inhabitant of your inner being, always available to give spiritual guidance.

You may now wish to converse directly with your Great Friend. I can give only suggestions as to what you may wish to ask or say.

You may want to ask how to live life with proper attention to spiritual reality. Listen to the answer carefully so that you can learn to distinguish the true voice of spiritual wisdom from the promptings of the ego.

To test whether the voice you hear is authentic, examine carefully the advice you are given. Does it seem self-aggrandizing? Does it suggest, for example, that your spiritual life will be on course when you are able to heal people, find the right mate, or manifest abundance?

If so, beware. You may be hearing the voice of spiritual materialism, which disguises in noble-sounding terms accomplishments that are really for your personal benefit.

If, on the other hand, your inner voice suggests actions that are of service to others and ways of being that increase your kindness and compassion and that make you more sensitive to the world's pain and to recognizing the Godseed in others, then the voice you hear is probably trustworthy.

You may also wish to ask your inner guide about developing your own spiritual practices. Having explored a few of the forms, you may now have a clearer knowing of

183

whether you're best suited to communing with nature, drawing, writing poetry, dancing, drumming, or sitting quietly in meditation.

Perhaps your practice is a combination of these, plus other activities known only to you. Ask your inner guide what you should do each day or how to improve practices that you are presently engaged in. Observe the images that come into your mind.

Your inner guide can also help you know how to create a sacred space in your home. You may be moved to turn a small table or dresser top into an altar by placing on it objects from nature—a plant, a vase of flowers, a special stone.

You may even wish to add pictures or symbols that relate to spiritual forces or figures that mean a lot to you—a picture of an angel or deity or spiritual teacher, an image or small statue, a shell, a candle.

You might also ask about ways of communicating with Spirit. Perhaps your Great Friend will suggest writing to a spiritual guide each day in your journal.

For years I wrote daily on my computer to an inner guide, who for me took the form of the Greek goddess Athena. What was most intriguing was that Athena always answered. Though I was "writing" both sides of the dialogue, it often seemed as if my local mind had bridged to Great Mind and that what was "written back" exceeded what I thought I knew.

The Great Friend can also counsel you on living a more spiritual life, one in which everyday acts are made sacred by attention to Source.

Perhaps you will be advised to imagine that the water of your shower is pouring down blessings and cleansing light, not only washing away physical impurities but also refreshing your emotions and thoughts and spirit.

Perhaps you will be inspired to make meals occasions of gratitude, celebrations of the abundance of life in all its forms.

The Great Friend also knows how you can best sustain a state of being in the Divine Presence.

You may be reminded that Christians repeat the Jesus Prayer over and over in their minds until it is spinning within them almost constantly: "Lord Jesus Christ, have mercy upon me." Or that Buddhists use much the same technique with a mantra like "Om mani padme hum."

Ask your Great Friend what your mantra should be, and don't be surprised at the answer.

Remember the story of the Jewish grandma who took up yoga and started chanting a mantra. Somewhere she had picked up the idea that a mantra should be "Indian."

When her spiritually sophisticated grandson visited, he was stunned and more than a little amused to hear her chanting, "Cheyenne . . . Cheyenne."

"Listen, darling," she said, when he told her that it wasn't a chant from India that she had been intoning, "by me it's Indian, and by me it works!"

Because the survival part of our brain keeps us alert to danger, we have a strong tendency to dwell on negative thoughts and feelings. Mantras, chants, and zikkrs fill up the mind with positive ideas and emotions, pushing out fear, anger, suspicion, jealousy, and other negative states.

Most important, ask your Great Friend the question that always arises when we are in a positive state of communion with Spirit: What service to the world can I give?

If an answer doesn't appear right away, then just look around, see what needs to be done, and do it!

It is as simple as that.

Service—whether it is comforting a friend or saving the redwoods—will provide its own teachings, far more than anything that you will find in this or any book.

These kinds of spiritual work, as well as other practices that might be suggested to you now or later by your Great Friend, will go far toward peeling away your brain cataracts and letting your Higher Self shine.

Your Friend leads you now to a path that brings you to the very center of the Rose. You move into a dazzling darkness in which it seems that everything is contained.

You have only to think of something and it appears. You have entered the Mind of the Maker—the Creative Force at the center of all there is.

Realities sweep through—stars and starfish, icebergs and ice cream, mountains and microchips, dolphins and daisies. Creation in its unending abundance.

Through it all, beneath it all, creating and sustaining it all, the Presence of Love.

Love that is tender and raging, always yearning and utterly complete.

Love that burns in our marrow, lures us into mystery, forgives our unskilled behavior, calls us into greatness.

Love that is ascending prayer and descending grace.

Love that moves the sun and all the stars.

Love that is the heartbeat of Eternity in time.

In the presence of such Love, your heart dissolves its fortress walls so that the Beloved may enter.

There is, for now, no more seeking. You are Home, at home in a sacred place that has always been within you. You had simply forgotten the way.

Here in the Home Place, you rest at the Hearth of Love. You understand as you never have before that your heart is part of Great Heart. Your mind, part of Great Mind. Your soul, part of Great Soul.

You and Everything have become water poured into Water.

You and the Divine have become one taste.

"Thank you," you whisper, for gratitude both given and received is here at the center of it all.

187

Your visit to the spiritual realm is ending. Or rather, it is beginning, for from this moment you are always connected, always Home.

Leaving the center of the Rose, you and the Friend retrace the spiral path through the heavenly petals. A wisp of spiritual pollen clings to you, a gift from the center of Creation, the center of the Rose. By its slight stickiness, you understand that you are, now and always, ready to be pollinated by the endless energy of Spirit.

You begin your journey back to your everyday life, passing through the sheet of water that marks the doorway to the Realm of the Spirit.

Traveling up the steep walk, you reach the door to the Realm of Myth and Symbol. It is inscribed with the story of your future. Watch its changing images for a few minutes and see what stories emerge. If you think the question, "What will happen if I take this path?" the mythic door may answer, showing you images of your life's journey as stories and symbols.

Moving up and around the interior pathway, you come to the mirrored door to the Realm of the Psyche. You peer into it but see no face or form, only light. After your visit to the spiritual realm, you are filled with light.

You reach the door to the Realm of the Senses. It echoes forth celebrational music in your honor.

With buoyant step, you move upward until, once again, you climb out of the entrance to the interior mountain. Picking up the stone tablet to cover the opening, you find to your delight that you can read the inscription:

NOW, YOU ARE MORE.

🐚 CULTIVATING EVERYDAY PASSION

Now the cat is out of the bag. With your senses tuned and your psyche primed, with a mythic path beneath your feet and the immensity of Spirit holding it all in Love, your life can be your work of art, your great creation, your everyday passion.

You have come a long way to reach this place. Chances are you have spent what seems like lifetimes yearning for something or someone to carry you home to who and what you really are.

Now it's your choice. The Home place you have longed for has always been within you. Think back over your travels—the inner landscapes you have explored, the special people you have met, the sensory and emotional riches you have experienced, the stories you have made your own, the Creator you discovered yourself to be. The great Kingdom within is your birthright, your splendid inheritance.

All that is required now is that you continue to till the soil of your soul. Just as you would not neglect seeds that you planted with the hope that they will bear vegetables and fruits and flowers, so you must attend to and nourish the garden of your becoming.

How can you do this? First, don't put this book away on a shelf. Keep it out where you can't miss it. Dip into it as often as you can for joy, for relaxation, as well as for learning, healing, service. Think of it as a Traveler's Guide Home, with useful maps and lists of What's Where and How to Get from Here to There.

On a day when you are feeling dim, go into the sensory realm and burnish your senses until they shine. Meet with cooks and musicians, painters and snifters, and those for whom touch is the road to glory. Let these inner guides give you back the world in its wonder.

Should you be feeling ill, visit again with the inner Healer and rediscover ways to embrace health. Remember the wise and willing crew you've always had but rarely have met. Above all, stay close to the Friend, your Essential Self, for this one knows who you really are and what you may yet become.

If you are feeling low and without purpose, go mythic! Let your mind give you a story, one you may already know or one that your mind discloses, and journey with it on the high road to adventure and transformation. You have within you a thousand heroic stories. Return to your life with the knowledge that you are living a Great Story, the next chapter of which is just now unfolding.

And when Spirit calls, answer. The spiritual realm is the source of all the others. There you return to the heart place of your Home's Home. There you are deepened and given the pattern as well as the purpose that guides your higher service in the world.

Now you have a passion for the possible. Now you can live the life you were meant to live. So just do it!

❧ Acknowledgments

This book had its inception as an hour-long program for PBS. I am extremely grateful to my producers and co-developers, Catherine Tatge, Dominique Lasseur, and Kenneth Cavander for working so long and hard with me to create what became an unusual and provocative piece of television viewing.

I want to thank Joe Durepos who urged me to write this book and who got it into the right hands at the right time with just the right presentation. His energy and dedication are mythic. Brenda Rosen, my magnificent in-house editor, gave constant suggestions and feedback as we worked together to create an evocative way of presenting the work and research of three decades.

Without her insights and critiques, this book would be much the poorer.

John Loudon, my editor at HarperSanFrancisco, offered apt and incisive editing and put me back on track when I was wandering far afield as is my wont. His associate, Karen Levine, was always present and available for help and information. And Priscilla Stuckey remains the finest copyeditor I know. Unlike some other publishing houses, HarperSanFrancisco keeps their authors up-to-date on all developments and partners them thoroughly in the enterprise of making a good book.

Peggy Nash Rubin added clarity and her own special genius to the development of the manuscript. My business manager, Fonda Joyce, and my assistant, Marie Joerss, were willing and valuable guinea pigs for the material presented here. I especially appreciate their original and refreshing take on arcane subjects. I am grateful, too, to the students of the 1997 Mystery School, who were the first to hear and try out this presentation of working with the four levels of consciousness. Their responses have been invaluable. And Betty Rothenberger, again, as with almost all of my previous books, has lent her fine eye and keen ear to the deepening and refinement of this work.

And finally, much gratitude to my husband, Robert Masters, for his ingenuity in thought, word, and deed.

193

For further information concerning Jean Houston's seminars, books, and tapes please write to her at Box 3300, Pomona, New York 10970.

Her website can be found at http://www.jeanhouston.org